FU

A **Better Homes and Gardens.** Book
An Imprint of
△▽○
HMH

Lyons
122 Broad Street
Lyons, New York 14489

Published by:
Houghton Mifflin Harcourt
Boston • New York
www.hmhco.com

For information about permission to reproduce selections from this book, write to Permissions, Houghton Mifflin Harcourt Publishing Company, 215 Park Avenue South, New York, New York 10003.

The publisher and author make no representations or warranties with respect to the accuracy or completeness of the contents of this work and specifically disclaim all warranties, including without limitation warranties of fitness for a particular purpose. No warranty may be created or extended by sales or promotional materials. The advice and strategies contained herein may not be suitable for every situation. This work is sold with the understanding that the publisher is not engaged in rendering legal, accounting, or other professional services. If professional assistance is required, the services of a competent professional person should be sought. Neither the publisher nor the author shall be liable for damages arising here from. The fact that an organization or Website is referred to in this work as a citation and/or a potential source of further information does not mean that the author or the publisher endorses the information the organization or Website may provide or recommendations it may take. Further, readers should be aware that Websites listed in this work may have changed or disappeared between when this work was written and when it is read.

TRADEMARKS: All trademarks are the property of their respective owners. Houghton Mifflin Harcourt is not associated with any product or vendor mentioned in this book.

Library of Congress Control Number available from the publisher upon request.
ISBN: 978-0-544-48133-6 (pbk); 978-0-544-48134-3 (ebk)
Printed in the United States of America
DOW 10 9 8 7 6 5 4 3 2 1
4500543405

NOTE TO THE READERS: Due to differing conditions, tools, and individual skills, Houghton Mifflin Harcourt assumes no responsibility for any damages, injuries suffered, or losses incurred as a result of following the information published in this book. Before beginning any project, review the instructions carefully, and if any doubts or questions remain, consult local experts or authorities. Because codes and regulations vary greatly, you always should check with authorities to ensure that your project complies with all applicable local codes and regulations. Always read and observe all of the safety precautions provided by manufacturers of any tools, equipment, or supplies, and follow all accepted safety procedures.

BETTER HOMES AND GARDENS® MAGAZINE
Executive Vice President, Creative Content Leader: Gayle Goodson Butler
Executive Editor: Oma Blaise Ford
Creative Director: Michael D. Belknap

BETTER HOMES AND GARDENS®
150+ QUICK & EASY FURNITURE PROJECTS
Contributing Editor and Writer: Pamela Porter
Contributing Designer: Kristin Cleveland
Contributing Copy Editor: Carrie Schmitz
Cover Photographer: Cameron Sadeghpour
Cover Designer: Leslie Poyzer

SPECIAL INTEREST MEDIA
Group Editorial Leader: Doug Kouma
Content Director, Home Design: Jill Waage
Deputy Content Director, Home Design: Karman Hotchkiss
Senior Design Director: Gene Rauch
Assistant Managing Editor: Jennifer Speer Ramundt
Business Director: Janice Croat

MEREDITH NATIONAL MEDIA GROUP
President: Tom Harty
President, Women's Lifestyle: Tomas Witschi
Chairman and Chief Executive Officer: Stephen M. Lacy

HOUGHTON MIFFLIN HARCOURT
Vice President and Publisher: Natalie Chapman
Editorial Director: Cindy Kitchel
Executive Editor, Brands: Anne Ficklen
Managing Editor: Marina Padakis Lowry
Production Editor: Donna Wright
Production Director: Tom Hyland
Senior Production Coordinator: Kimberly Keifer

CONTRIBUTING PHOTOGRAPHERS
Adam Albright, King Au, Karla Conrad, Kim Cornelison, Jacob Fox, Kathryn Gamble, Kritsada, Scott Little, Steven Mcdonald, Mathew Mead, Blaine Moats, Cameron Sadeghpour, Greg Scheidemann, Jim Smith, Werner Straube, Jay Wilde

CONTRIBUTING DESIGNERS & STYLISTS
Karen Brady, Beth Eslinger, Kate Carter Frederick, Jodi Mensing Harris, Adam Holt, Cathy Kramer, Meredith Ladik, Katie Leporte, John Loeke, Mathew Mead, Jean Schissel Norman, Angie Packer, Pamela Porter, Leslie Poyzer, Sara Reimer, Margaret Sindelar, Arin Wiebers, Jeni Wright

welcome

If you like to reimagine your home and furnishings, then you've come to the right place. Whether you're a daily DIYer or an occasional weekend warrior, the following pages offer fresh, doable ideas for turning tired furnishings into one-of-a-kind creations. Eager to replace that chair? Ready to discard that dresser? Consider a redo before you buy new.

With just a few tools, a few hours, and a few bucks, the possibilities are endless. Discover the satisfaction you'll feel (and bragging rights you'll earn) after giving new life to an old relic. Let these inspiring projects, clever techniques, and helpful tips get your creative juices flowing and your furniture makeovers going. So what are you waiting for? Let the transformations begin!

HOW TO USE
this book

QUICK PROJECTS

Crunched for time? You can still tackle many furniture redo projects. A stopwatch symbol identifies projects in this book that can be done in 2 hours or less.

INEXPENSIVE PROJECTS

Don't let a tight budget put an end to your creative endeavors. Look for this piggy bank symbol and know a project like this won't cost you more than $50 for materials.

TOOL FRIENDLY PROJECTS

Think you need a slew of tools to make over furniture? That's certainly not the case for projects identified with this symbol, which take just one or two.

150+ Quick & Easy Furniture Projects

table of contents

Living Rooms

One of the best places to showcase your *pride-and-joy* projects is a *living room*. In this public space, furniture makeovers big and small can be admired by all and spark interesting *topics of conversation*.

When this bland **ottoman** needed a little boost, decorative upholstery nails came to the rescue. Gem-like nailheads were applied to the side of the ottoman, *this photo*, in an overlapping oval design. Select an ottoman with a firm frame, and use needle-nose pliers to hold the nailheads as you tap them in using a rubber mallet. To ensure even spacing, measure and mark each nail placement.

This thrift store score featured delightful lines, but the charm stopped there. The chair's dated burgundy upholstery was rescued with Chalk Paint in a fresh aqua hue, *this photo*. The flower painted over top mimics a vintage paint-by-number design, but its large scale offers modern appeal.

Painted Upholstery

The idea of painting upholstery might seem shocking, but the right materials can yield amazing results.

materials

- Clean cloth
- Chalk Paint
- Paintbrushes
- Fine-grit sandpaper
- Tack cloth
- Paint pen
- Flower pattern
- Clear wax
- Painter's tape

instructions

1 Use a wet cloth to dampen the chair upholstery fabric in workable sections (**a**). Apply paint to the fabric (**b**). If needed for complete coverage, apply a second coat while the first is still damp. Continue to dampen and paint fabric in workable sections until the surface is covered. Let dry. Sand the fabric lightly (**c**) then wipe with a tack cloth.

2 Find a flower image online and enlarge it to desired size. Cut the flower into paint-by-number type shapes. Tape one shape at a time to the chair and trace using a paint pen (**d**).

3 Fill in the shapes with desired paint colors (**e**). Let dry. Use a paint pen to outline some of the shapes and add numbers, if desired. Apply a clear wax coating to seal the fabric.

4 Before painting the frame, use painter's tape to mask the fabric (**f**). Apply paint to the wood frame (**g**), allowing some of the original wood finish to show. Let dry.

5 Sand the wood to achieve a distressed finish (**h**). Wipe with a tack cloth, then apply a clear wax to protect the finish.

materials

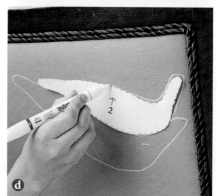

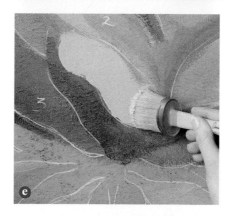

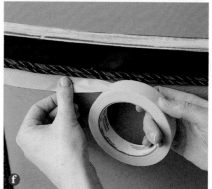

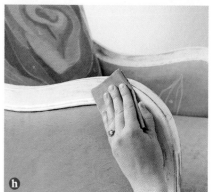

Ribbon Stripes

Colorful ribbons dress up furniture just as easily as they do a gift-wrapped package. In this little nook, strips of grosgrain ribbon highlight a wing chair's curvy silhouette, *below* and *right*. Measure the surface before cutting ribbon to desired lengths. Double-sided fusible adhesive tape makes it easy to adhere the ribbon without messing with glue. Apply the tape to the back of the ribbon in manageable strips. Then place the ribbon tape side down on the chair, and secure using an iron and following tape manufacturer's instructions to set the tape. Use different widths and patterns of ribbon to boost the style. The pink side table also flaunts a ribbon accent, applied with the same fusible tape and coordinating grosgrain ribbon.

Use ribbon to embellish accessories like this lampshade or a pillow.

before

Slipcover Rescue

Oftentimes old furniture is well made but just looks too dated to live with. This vintage slipper chair, *above*, is a perfect example, featuring sturdy construction but unsightly fabric. Purchased slipcovers are a quick-fix alternative to reupholstering; they come in basic styles to fit many standard furnishings, such as this chair. For a personal touch, add a fabric or ribbon band around the bottom of the slipcover and a feedsack or other interesting fabric strip to its seat back. Here, rickrack adds a nice border and covers the seams.

TIP: *If you prefer a no-sew project, use fabric glue or fusible adhesive to secure fabric accents to a slipcover.*

Easy Cover

This chair makeover, *above*, features an easy cushion re-cover and paint job on the frame. The seat and back cushions were removed and re-covered with blue fabric. Before replacing them, the frame was painted using a semigloss paint. For an additional layer of pattern, pieces of fabric were cut and hemmed to use as tie-on slipcovers. This slipcover reverses to another pattern, *left*, so it's easy to change on a whim. If you don't want to sew, use fusible tape or fabric glue to hem edges and attach ribbons. Tie-on slipcovers aren't just for furniture in need of a drastic makeover. Try them on your favorite seating to add a temporary dash of color or a seasonal touch.

Paint an old metal stool and repurpose it as a petite side table.

Go casual with denim upholstery fashioned from recycled jeans. The chair's charming frame was painted white, and the original red faux-velvet fabric gave way to denim featuring a herringbone strip that gives the classic chair more modern appeal.

Sew a Herringbone Pattern

Random widths and offset construction make this herringbone variation easy to create.

materials

- Denim scraps
- Cutting mat
- Rotary cutter
- Sewing machine
- Thread
- Iron and ironing board
- Acrylic ruler

instructions

1 Cut denim into strips about 2–3 inches wide by 6–7 inches long. Stagger the strips (*a*) and sew them together using ½-inch seam allowances. Iron seams open (*b*).

2 Place the sewn strip on a cutting mat, aligning the top edge parallel to the top of the mat. Place an acrylic ruler at a 30- to 45-degree angle and cut (*c*) to make the sides straight. Use the angled lines on the mat as a guide (*d*). Repeat on the opposite side of the strip so you have clean edges on both sides.

3 Repeat steps 1 and 2, but stagger the denim strips so they will be angled in the opposite direction of the first strip (*e*).

4 Place sewn strips right sides together, and sew one long side using a ½-inch seam allowance (*f*). Press open and sew the finished stripe between two pieces of denim to use to upholster the chair seat.

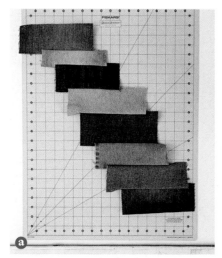

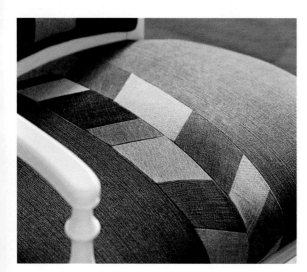

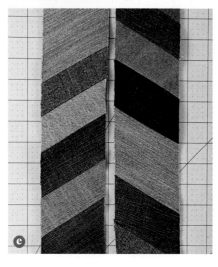

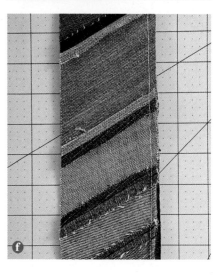

Wicker and other woven furnishings aren't just for the outdoors. Bring these natural wonders inside to give warmth and texture to a room. This chair's brown finish was in disrepair, but it looks fresh and new after a few coats of paint, *this photo*, and an updated cushion, *opposite*.

Painted Cushion

An easy painted pattern can give a plain seat cushion designer style in no time.

materials

- Thin painter's or crafts tape
- Clean cloth
- Artist's paintbrush
- Chalk Paint or fabric paint

instructions

1 Apply strips of ¼-inch-wide tape about 2 inches apart across the seat cushion (*a*). Use a wet cloth to dampen one taped-off strip at a time (*b*).

2 Use a medium-size artist's brush to paint slanted lines across the dampened strip, being careful to not let the lines extend past the tape. Repeat with the adjoining strip, dampening the area and then painting lines angled the opposite way of the first strip (*c*). Continue in this manner across the entire cushion.

3 Remove the tape (*d*) when the paint is partially dry but still tacky. Let dry completely. Use painter's tape to mask under the cushion buttons, then paint the buttons a dark teal color.

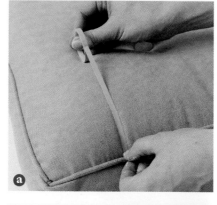

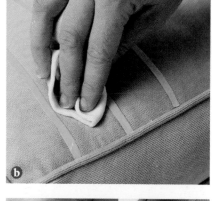

tips & tricks

When giving cushions or accent pillows a new look with paint or other embellishments, apply a different style, color, or design to the back so you can flip them over for a quick change.

before

This little duo wasn't always so delightful. The chair was a $10 garage sale score, and the stool was rescued from a Dumpster. Both needed a fresh look, and reupholstering was the best answer. By selecting coordinating fabrics, the re-covered chair and stool look like a matching set. Consider durable, easy-to-clean coverings like vinyl for footstools and upholstery-weight, stain-resistant fabric for chairs and sofas.

Paint the tips of furniture legs to mimic classic metal caps.

Upholster Like a Pro

Don't be intimidated to tackle an upholstery project.
Start small and follow these steps.

materials

- Camera or notepaper and pencil
- Marking pen
- Needle-nose pliers
- Scissors
- ½-inch batting
- Staple gun and staples, ⅜- or ⁵⁄₁₆-inch
- Upholstery fabric
- Straight pins
- ⁵⁄₃₂-inch welt cord
- Sewing machine
- Upholstery-weight thread
- Tack strips
- Fabric glue (optional)
- Upholstery tacks or nailhead trim (optional)

instructions

1 Take photographs or detailed notes as you disassemble the chair as a guide for reassembly. Mark the placement of the pieces, indicating top and bottom as they are removed. Save welting and tack strips to measure for new pieces. Remove each piece of upholstery by carefully loosening tacks or staples with pliers. Try not to rip the fabric, as you will use the pieces as a pattern. Use scissors to separate fabric pieces at any seams.

2 Remove old batting from chair back and seat if it's worn. Repair springs and webbing if needed. If needed, sand, prime, and paint the chair frame and let dry. Cut a piece of batting to cover the chair back and another for the seat. Staple each piece in place, folding neatly around the corners (**a**).

3 Lay original upholstery pieces, wrong side up, on the wrong side of new fabric, paying attention to the grain and pattern. Pin in place and cut out, leaving 2–3 inches of excess fabric beyond the original fabric (**b**). Transfer markings for direction and placement onto new pieces.

4 Place base fabric pieces on the frame, pull taut, and staple in place on the apron front and back (**c**). Trim excess fabric.

5 Using the old pieces as a guide for length needed, cut bias strips and welt cord to fit the chair. Join strips using diagonal seams, then fold them around the cord and use a zipper foot to sew close to the cord.

6 Pin the side panel to the seat fabric, making any necessary adjustments to the fit or pattern placement. Mark the position for the bottom welting, remove the fabric, and sew the welting to the right side of the panel, at top and where marked near the bottom, starting and ending at the back.

7 Holding right side of panel up against the seat, staple the top welting in place around the seat (**d**). Add a tack strip around the panel top against the welting and staple in place.

8 Fold the side panel down over the tack strip, pull tight, and staple in place to the underside of the chair, with the bottom welting fitting snugly along the edge. Snip notches in the fabric underneath the seat as you smooth around corners.

9 Place back panel in position and fold right side over the top of the chair back. Apply a tack strip to the top of the back rear and staple in place (**e**). Fold the panel back over the strip and pull tight toward the bottom of the chair back. Fold bottom edge under and staple to underside of the chair back. Use fabric glue or decorative upholstery tacks to secure excess fabric to the back of the chair (**f**).

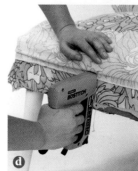

tips & tricks

Purchase an inexpensive magnetic pin wand to make it easier to find and pick up all those tiny staples, pins, and tacks.

Made to Suit

Coffee tables are ideal makeover candidates and can be delightfully versatile to meet a variety of living room needs.

Create Seating One long bench or a few smaller benches or cubes can serve as extra seating.

Offer Mobility Add casters to make a small or large coffee table easy to move out of the way.

Save Space Nesting tables that tuck into one another save space when not in use.

Increase Storage Who can't use more storage? Look for furniture with shelves and drawers.

Go for Comfort Find a table with an upholstered top you can re-cover or a hard surface you can upholster to serve as a foot rest.

Add Originality If you're looking for a one-of-a-kind creation, select a piece not originally or commonly used as a coffee table, such as a boot bench, and repurpose it as such.

Stenciled Style

Charming and versatile, this vintage piece, ***above***, was originally a dining table. The legs were cut down to achieve a comfortable coffee-table height. The drop leaves are a nice bonus: When propped up, they more than double the tabletop surface, which is nice when entertaining. But they drop conveniently out of the way for everyday use.

Once the legs are cut, the table was primed and painted a tomato-red hue. Next, a modern bird stencil was applied to the tabletop using a darker red color, ***right***. The tone-on-tone scheme creates a subtle and sophisticated design. The same red hue was applied to the table's beveled edge to accentuate its delightful figure. A clear sealer protects the flock.

TIP: *Standard coffee-table height is 16–18 inches, but it should ultimately suit your needs. Use cardboard boxes to experiment with various heights before cutting a table down to size.*

Repurposed Crates

Looking for a clever coffee-table idea that won't break the bank? Old or new, inexpensive wooden crates can be arranged to make great modular furniture, *this photo*. For this coffee-table design, be sure crates are identical in size. Paint or stain them, or leave them as found. Use screws to attach six crates together (back to back and side to side) so fronts are facing out as shown here. Cut a piece of plywood as a base, screw the crates on top, then add casters.

Table Cover

Sometimes a piece of furniture you don't need can be converted into a piece you do need. In this case, a small writing desk was transformed into a charming bench-style ottoman, *right*, by cutting about 8 inches off the legs and slipcovering the top. Underneath this slipcover is a foam cushion to give the table a padded top for resting feet or holding a serving tray for flowers or refreshments.

TIP: *For a supereasy variation of this makeover, skip the slipcover and pad altogether, and you'll have a nice wooden coffee table instead.*

before

A large monogram or other stylish wall decal can eliminate the need for pricey artwork.

Decal Embellishment

Peel-and-stick decals aren't just for walls—they're an easy way to add fun style to plain furniture. Typically made of vinyl, decals are easy to apply and reasonably priced. Almost all are removable, and most are even repositionable so they can be reused elsewhere. Some sellers even allow you to select the size and colors. A large white decal in a lace doily design was cut into quarters and applied to the tops of four square tables, *left* and **below**, to appear to be one large coffee table when placed together.

tips & tricks

When applying a large decal, it's easiest to have an extra pair of hands so one person can peel off the backing while the other smooths the decal in place.

Luxurious or laid back? Create a coffee table that's just your style.

Gold Leafing

For a little glam and glimmer, accentuate a favorite furniture piece with gold leaf, ***above*** and ***left.*** Purchase a metal leafing kit that includes adhesive, sealer, and gold-leaf sheets. Clean and sand the surface to be embellished. Porous surfaces may need to be sealed before you apply metal leaf. Brush on adhesive in a smooth coat and let dry just until tacky or according to manufacturer's instructions. Apply metal leaf by gently smoothing it over areas of adhesive. Smooth out any wrinkles with your fingertips or a clean, dry paintbrush. Apply clear sealer right away so the gold doesn't oxidize.

TIP: *Gold leaf is very delicate and tears easily. Once it touches the adhesive, you can't remove it, so be sure to apply the adhesive and leaf exactly where you want it. Use painter's tape to mask areas if needed.*

Painted Runner

Mimic a chic table runner by stenciling a patterned stripe on a coffee table, ***above*** and ***left***. For a whitewashed effect, water down the paint slightly to allow some of the wood grain and texture to show through. When dry, sand lightly. Apply a clear sealer or wax coating over top to protect the design.

before

Country Charm

One unfinished coffee table can take on many different looks. For a touch of country, try a weathered finish and fabric skirt, *above.* Prime the table, paint it red, and let dry. Rub a candle over edges and other areas you want the red to show through. Apply a blue top coat, *left,* and let dry. Use fine-grit sandpaper to lightly sand through the blue paint to expose the red paint where desired.

For the skirt panels, cut fabric to fit the four open areas between the table legs, allowing extra for hems on all sides and desired gathering horizontally. Sew the soft strip of hook-and-loop tape to the top of the backside of each panel, gathering slightly as you go. Stick the adhesive side of hook-and-loop tape to the coffee table above the openings, and attach the panels by joining the tapes.

Traditional Lines

Strike a traditional note with a shimmering lattice motif atop a rich chocolate brown hue, *above,* chosen to mimic a stained finish. Prime the table, paint brown, and let dry.

Place a lattice-pattern stencil on the top, and use a stencil brush to apply gold paint. Keep repositioning the stencil until the entire tabletop is painted. Paint a border of gold around the pattern, as well as around the table edges and drawer fronts, using painter's tape as needed, *left*. Complete the look by installing brass hardware.

TIP: *To help ensure success with your stencil, look for stencil tips in the Tools & Techniques section starting on page 178.*

Cottage Chic

Shapely shelf brackets and beaded board from a home center give this table, *above,* sweet style. Use wood glue and screws to secure four shelf brackets to the table and legs (two on each side of the table). Cut beaded board and cap molding to fit the top of the table, mitering the ends of the molding and attaching both using wood glue, *right.*

Fill original drawer-knob holes with wood filler. Let dry, sand, then wipe with a tack cloth. Prime then paint the table. When dry, measure and drill drawer fronts for two knobs each, then install milk-glass knobs in a vintage-green hue.

Modern Lines

Contrasting colors, woven texture, and a bit of metal lend modern appeal to this makeover, *above.* Jump-start the redo by sawing off the bottoms of the legs where they start to taper. Stain and seal all but the tabletop.

Cut grass cloth to fit the top and drawer fronts, and attach using spray adhesive. Cut angled aluminum trim with mitered corners, *right,* to fit the tabletop edges. Install it using metal adhesive, clamping until dry. Lightly sand the aluminum, file the corners, wipe clean, and coat with a clear lacquer. For a final touch of metal, add silver casters and statement drawer pulls.

Cabinet Table

Here's a makeover that comes straight from the kitchen. This coffee table, *right,* is crafted from two kitchen cabinets that were being discarded during a kitchen remodel. Screw the cabinets together and paint.

To bring the cabinets to coffee-table height, construct a base from 2×4 boards and face with veneer. Attach the cabinets to the base. For a tabletop, cut a piece of medium-density fiberboard (MDF) to overhang the cabinets an inch on all sides. Paint the surface aqua blue and top with a polyurethane finish. When dry, attach top to cabinets. Add showy, contrasting knobs.

Secure a board or small shelf inside a frame to create a display ledge.

tips & tricks
Replacing old cabinet door hinges can be tricky (and expensive). Be sure to keep all hinges and mark which door they go on before removing them to paint the piece.

On Display

Priceless collections aren't the only things worthy of displaying under glass. Wallpaper remnants and art paper are inexpensive ways to add color and pattern to a room. Cut strips of paper to varying lengths and arrange on the tabletop. These strips, *left,* are placed in an offset brick pattern, but you can arrange a different pattern or even place them randomly. Secure the paper to the tabletop using decoupage medium. When dry, place a piece of glass over top. A glass store can cut glass to custom sizes and finish with a smooth beveled edge. Selecting tempered glass will cost more, but because it is stronger and safer if it breaks, it's worth every penny.

Select one modern furnishing as a statement piece in an otherwise traditional room.

Give a gaudy gold frame stunning new style by painting just part of it white.

Tiled Top

Abandoned on a curb, this sturdy sideboard needed a complete facelift. The dated finials were cut off, then the piece was primed and painted blue, *opposite*. A pretty tile mosaic top adds colorful style. Use damaged dishes and wear safety goggles when creating mosaic-tile pieces. Place dishes on a protected work surface, cover them with a towel, and use a hammer to break into small pieces.

Tape off an area the size of your tabletop, and arrange tile pieces inside the tape until you're happy with the design. Keep the distance between pieces consistent, *above*. Tape off the top rim of the table to ensure a smooth grout line. Cut double-sided peel-and-stick mastic to fit the tabletop; remove paper backing and stick on. Remove paper from top of the mastic, then transfer the tile pieces to the mastic, pressing each piece down firmly. When all pieces are in place, spread premixed white grout over them using a trowel, pressing grout into spaces between the tiles. Remove excess grout using a trowel, and wipe clean using water and a sponge before the grout dries on the tiles. Drawer fronts, *above right,* were decoupaged using lace fabric and decoupage medium.

TIP: *When tiling a tabletop, look for furniture that has a recessed top. Otherwise, you'll need to create one by framing the top with trim boards.*

before

More Ideas
Before settling on this makeover, these alternative ideas were considered. Which do you like best?

Faux Paper Tiling Tile and grout add a lot of weight to a piece. You can get a similar mosaic look by using paper and glue.

Color-Blocking Each of the three levels could be painted a different color and the legs a fourth color.

Skirting These shelves provide lots of storage, but everything is in view. Fabric panels attached using hook-and-loop tape would conceal clutter on the bottom two shelves while adding softness, pattern, and color to a room.

Metal Leafing The six turned posts beg for attention. Gold or silver leaf would accentuate them beautifully.

Repurposing With its symmetrical design, this sideboard could make a nice double-sink vanity in a master bathroom.

Nailhead Glamour

Jewel-like nailheads luxe up any furnishing that needs a flashy touch. This focal-point cabinet, *left*, started as a bargain chinoiserie reproduction with flat door fronts perfect for applying ornamentation.

Pick a base color like semigloss white that shows off the design. Instead of drilling and hammering nailheads, which can be tedious, find a faux alternative. Glue on silver-spray-painted round wood plugs or three-dimensional silver nailhead stickers available at crafts stores.

Be tame with the design and simply outline the edges, or have fun and create a geometric pattern, strips, a monogram, or a flourish, *above*. Lightly draw more complex designs on the surface using a pencil, then add your embellishment.

Mirrored Table

With its lovely curves and beveled edges, this demilune table, *right*, begged for a showstopping finish. To achieve this mirrored look, sand and prime the table. When dry, brush the legs and the beveled edges with silver leaf, and seal them with polyurethane. Trace kraft-paper patterns of the curvy tabletop and side panels. For the tabletop, have ¼-inch-thick mirror cut to fit and seamed to ensure a smooth edge. Have the side panels cut from ⅛-inch-thick mirror. Attach the mirrors using mirror mastic adhesive. Adhere ready-made round mirrored coasters to the center of each side.

TIP: *As an alternative to silver leaf, you could use metallic silver spray paint.*

before

Re-Cover an Ottoman

Give an ottoman a whole new look using entry-level upholstery skills, minimal tools, and no sewing!

materials

- Electric drill and drill bits
- Flat-head screwdriver
- Scissors
- Muslin
- Upholstery fabric
- Quilt batting
- Marking pen
- Staple gun and staples
- Fusible interfacing
- Fabric glue
- Decorative embellishments (optional)

instructions

1 Remove ottoman feet and mounting hardware with drill. Carefully remove fabric from ottoman, using a flat-head screwdriver if needed to loosen staples. Set the circle of old fabric on top of muslin and trace, adding 2 inches all around. Cut new fabric to the same size as the muslin. If high-density foam and batting are in good condition, leave them and just add a few layers of fresh quilt batting on top (***a***).

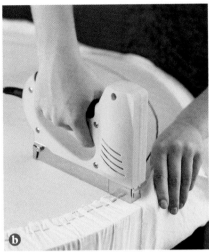

2 Using a marking pen, draw a guideline on the underside of the ottoman base that is 2 inches from the edge. Mark four even points on the circle, dividing it into quarters. Fold and press the muslin into fourths. Unfold, center and smooth muslin over the batting, turn upside down, then match up the folds in the muslin with the lines on the base. Start stapling the muslin around the base, keeping the folds aligned with the marker points (***b***).

3 Repeat Step 2 using upholstery fabric (***c***).

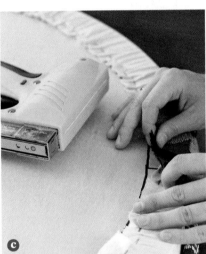

4 Add a decorative trim edge by allowing ¾ inch along the trim edge, positioning right sides together, then stapling through fusible interfacing to secure the trim in place (***d***).

5 Turn back the decorative edge and glue in place with fabric glue (***e***). Use fabric glue to secure decorative embellishments such as beads and sequins if desired.

6 Replace mounting hardware and ottoman feet (***f***).

If you want to try your hand at reupholstering, start with an ottoman. They are manageable and easy to re-cover in a few hours. And the results are sure to boost your confidence to try something more challenging.

before

Wallpaper and Curtains

There are endless ways to remake an unfinished bookcase. This cottage-style charmer, **right,** was primed and painted a creamy white hue. When dry, a subtle wallpaper was added to the inside back. Shelves on the lower part of the case are hidden behind café curtains shirred onto a tension rod. If you can't find curtains in just the right size, hem two fabric panels, incorporating a 1-inch rod pocket in the top of each.

If you want display items to pop more, use a wallpaper with more contrast.

Paint and Doors

This storage-savvy idea hides items behind closed doors, *above.*
Prime and paint the case and let dry. Use hinges to attach two
wood panels or shutters. These board-and-batten shutters
were custom-crafted (look online for sources), but if you're
handy, you could make your own. A forged-iron shutter bolt
keeps the shutters securely closed.

Stain and Shade

When staining unfinished wood, use a wood conditioner first.
This bookcase, *above,* was stained using an ebony gel stain,
which is easy to apply. When dry, install a roller shade inside
the frame at the top. Order a custom shade that is 1 inch
narrower than the width between the sides of the frame and
long enough to reach the bottom shelf. Add a decorative shade
pull, and you're ready to draw the shade to hide whatever
portion of the case you wish.

TIP: *Before staining wood, test the stain on a hidden
area first to make sure the color is what you expected.*

Dowel Table

With a few simple steps, basic dowels transform a purchased side table, *left*. Choose a table with clean, straight lines and a flat, wide top. Use wood glue to attach dowel pieces around the sides of the table, *below,* so they cover the sides and extend beyond the top by ¾ inch to create a raised border in which to arrange slices cut from various-size dowels. Cut ¾-inch slices from dowles in a random assortment of diameters, sanding rough edges as needed, then arrange the slices on the tabletop, starting with the largest dowels first and filling in with smaller ones. When happy with the arrangement, glue slices to the tabletop using wood glue. When dry, sand the top using a handheld sander to ensure a level surface. Spray the top and sides with a coat of clear sealer.

Cover tabletops with cork, bottle caps, cards or whatever else you can think of!

Yardstick Table

This table topper, *right*, really measures up! Find yardsticks at flea markets, antiques shops, or online. Select yardsticks of the same thickness. Secure them to the top of a purchased table using wood glue, letting the sticks overhang the edges and clamping until dry. Use a router to trim the sticks flush with the table edge, *above*, and then sand smooth. Seal with polyurethane if desired.

TIP: *Give new, unfinished wood yardsticks instant age by staining them. Experiment with light, dark, and color stains, mottling the color slightly. Complete the illusion by using sandpaper to weather the finish.*

Glossy turquoise paint refreshes a black metal lamp base.

Strip and Stencil

Say good-bye to this table's dated paint finish and hello to a sophisticated modern stencil, *right* and *below.* Original plans for stripping and staining this curvaceous piece were brought to a halt when less-than-perfect wood was revealed. But a pretty stencil over the wood surface let some wood finish show through while masking imperfections. The revelation turned out to be good fortune, resulting in a lovely little makeover.

Stripping Paint

*Prefer a wood finish? Uncover wood that's been
hidden for years under layers of paint.*

materials

- Drop cloth
- Paintbrush
- Wood stripper
- Putty knife
- Scrap bucket
- Wire-bristle brush
- Steel wool
- Mineral spirits
- Medium- and fine-grit sandpaper or sanding block
- Tack cloths

instructions

1 Place table on a drop cloth in a ventilated area. Use a
paintbrush to apply a thin layer of wood stripper (***a***). Once the
surface has bubbled, use a putty knife to scrape paint off flate
surfaces (***b***) and steel wool to remove paint from curved legs;
discard paint remnants in a scrap bucket. If needed, repeat
with a second coat of stripper (***c, d***).

2 Use a small wire-bristle brush to remove paint from
crevices. Using a piece of steel wool and rubbing with the
direction of the grain, wipe down the wood with mineral spirits
to remove stripper and paint residue. Let dry for 15 minutes.

3 Sand the table using medium-grit sandpaper or block (***e***),
moving with even pressure in the direction of the grain.
Wipe down with a tack cloth to remove dust. Sand again with
fine-grit sandpaper. Wipe with a clean tack cloth and the table
is ready to finish as you desire.

before

tips & tricks

When applying
polyurethane, stir it
well, but never shake
the can to mix it.
Shaking creates
bubbles that will
show up in your
final finish.

Marker Table

A faux bois pattern fancies up this cylindrical side table. Use a fine-point black Sharpie marker to sketch slightly wavy vertical lines along the side of the table from top to bottom, adding a swirly knot shape here and there to mimic wood grain. When the side is complete, extend each line over the top edge and along the tabletop surface, stopping 3–4 inches in from the edge. If you prefer, sketch the design with a pencil first, and then trace over the pencil lines using a marker.

TIP: *Experiment with different widths of marker on a piece of paper first. You might prefer thicker but fewer lines.*

Use markers to create doodle-inspired frames and artwork.

gallery of great ideas
Decals, decoupage, and more! Give these doable aha ideas a try today.

This little makeover, *above*, is as easy as peel and stick. Dress up accent furniture with vinyl decals—they're easy to find, inexpensive, and a snap to apply. Decals work on just about any smooth surface and enhance any style, including these clean-lined modern nesting tables. Best of all, most decals can be removed if you tire of the look.

Combine a collection of vintage benches to create a whole new idea. Look for wooden benches in a variety of finishes to coordinate with your space. Be sure they are all about the same depth. Stack them, playing with the arrangement to create various levels of shelves, *above*. Secure the benches together using screws, or leave them separate if you want flexibility to move them around.

Add a reflective surface to a side table, *above*, by having a mirror cut to fit the top. A table with a slight lip works best. Use acid-free adhesive to secure the mirror. Use stencil adhesive to secure a stencil on the mirror, and apply silver enamel paint using a stencil brush, stippling gently until the design is covered. Remove the stencil and let the paint cure for 21 days.

Perk up a plain bookcase using painted blocks of color, *above*. Remove shelves and use painter's tape to mask arrows on the back. Paint the space between each shelf a different color, using painter's tape to mask between colors. Paint the top of each shelf to match the color above it.

Make use of wallpaper scraps with a decoupage treatment. This hand-me-down side table, *above*, was updated with metallic paint and glaze before being decoupaged with paper blooms cut from a remnant of designer wallpaper.

Create a mobile game station by skirting a metal utility cart with fabric, *above*. Measure and hem a length of fabric to fit around the cart, then use adhesive-back hook-and-loop tape or strong magnets to secure it in place.

Remake a castoff with paint and a few upgrades. An old file cabinet sports modern style, *this photo*, when refreshed with silver-gray paint, new hardware, and wooden feet.

before

Small but Mighty
Snatch up petite wood cabinets whenever you get the chance. They are amazingly versatile and quick to redo. Other than the typical bedside or sofa side table, try them out here.

Laundry A small cabinet can tuck beside a washer or under a utility sink.

Entry Perfect for stowing seasonal and small items by the front or back door.

Basement Perch at the bottom of the steps or in a storage room to hold batteries or lightbulbs.

Office or Hobby Space Organize a slew of supplies that overflow from your desk drawers.

Garage Tuck away tools.

Kids Room Ideal for toys, collections, crafts supplies, and keepsakes.

Painted Cabinet

A top-to-bottom remake means an unsightly file cabinet is ready to relocate to the living room.

materials

- Drop cloth
- Wood filler
- Fine-grit sandpaper or sanding block
- Tack cloth
- Furniture feet
- Painter's tape
- Paintbrush or small paint roller
- Primer
- Paint
- Drawer pull

materials

instructions

1 Use a drop cloth to protect work surface. Remove cabinet hardware and fill holes with wood filler (**a**). Let set. Use sandpaper or a sanding block to sand all areas to be painted (**b**). Wipe with a tack cloth (**c**).

2 Remove drawers and casters. Install new furniture feet (**d**).

3 Use painter's tape to mask any areas of wood you want to keep exposed—like the bottom half of the drawer front on this cabinet (**e**). Using a paintbrush or roller and painting with the grain of the wood, apply primer to the cabinet (**e, f**). Let dry.

4 Painting with the grain of the wood (**g, h**), apply a top coat of semigloss latex paint using a paintbrush or roller. Apply two light coats of paint rather than one thick coat, and let dry between coats.

5 Remove any painter's tape while the paint is still tacky but not wet. When dry, install new drawer pull.

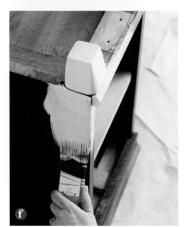

Kitchens & Dining Rooms

Rooms dedicated to prepping, serving, and entertaining deserve *special treatment.* These multitasking spaces require smart furnishings that perform yet flaunt *personal style.* Let these *project-packed* pages get your creative juices flowing.

Relocate a tool cart from the garage to the kitchen as an island, *this photo.* Carts come in an array of sizes to suit any space. Metal frames are convenient; they can hold magnetic hooks and spice jars. Cut a piece of butcher block to fit the top, and secure with construction adhesive.

Cocktail Cabinet

This castoff, *right,* had few redeeming qualities and was missing a shelf, but the petite size worked in its favor as a modest bar for a small space. The cabinet was painted semigloss white, and for durability the top was sealed with a water-base acrylic sealer. Metallic wallpaper covers the interior back, and new glass knobs replace the original wood ones, adding a festive sparkle. You could add casters to the legs to make it mobile.

In the opening below the drawer, a wineglass holder was installed, *below right,* and a coat hook secured to the side of the cabinet, *below,* holds a bar towel within easy reach.

TIP: *If you need a larger serving surface, cut a piece of medium-density fiberboard (MDF) to overhang the cabinet by about a foot on each side. Place it on top when entertaining, and stow it away when not.*

A narrow towel bar would also work here.

before

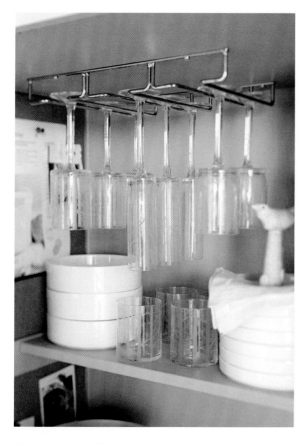

Alternate ways to achieve this X design: Use a paint pen or black string.

Beverage Center

Raise a glass to this all-you-need bar armoire, **right.** The transformation began by cutting the doors in half to open the top as a serving area. Adding crown molding to the top and a scrolled molding to the bottom dresses up the boxy shape. X-shape inserts in the lower half help sort wine bottles, napkins, and candles.

After a coat of blue paint, the armoire was outfitted with a slew of storage helpers. Cork on the inside door panels, **above right,** and cabinet sides post recipes for favorite concoctions. A wineglass holder, **above,** installed at the top maximizes space by freeing up valuable shelf space. For a decorative touch, knobs secured to the center of the cabinet doors are accentuated by painted dowels that form a classy X design.

before

Dress walls with floral or other natural motifs in keeping with an eco chic style.

Reed Effect

Vertical rows of dowels applied to the recessed areas of drawer fronts and cabinet doors give a plain console table a breezy, island-inspired vibe with reeded details, *left* and ***below.*** Pick a dowel diameter that best fits the depth of the recessed areas on your furniture piece, and measure and cut all the pieces to fit each area from top to bottom.

Before adhering the dowels, remove the drawers and doors, and lay the pieces on a work surface so the panels are flat. Coat the recessed areas with wood glue, and press the dowels side-by-side into the glue. Fill in odd gaps at the ends of the rows by readjusting the previous dowels. When dry, drill through dowels to install drawer pulls. If desired, apply a protective coating of clear acrylic sealer.

Hidden Storage

Fabric panels not only add color, pattern, and softness to this sideboard, *left,* but they also create a concealed storage area on the otherwise open shelf underneath. Cut and hem fabric to fit the side and front openings, creating a rod pocket at the top of each panel. Hang the panels from tension rods installed between the legs.

Before adding the fabric panels, the base of this sideboard was painted a yellow-green hue, and the top was given a metallic finish, *below left,* using a leafing kit. Apply the kit's adhesive to the tabletop, and let it sit 30 minutes. Place the leaf onto the adhesive, and brush gently with a dry paintbrush to burnish the leaf to the table and clear away loose pieces. Repeat with more leaf, overlapping and burnishing until the entire top is covered. Apply a coat of leaf sealer and let dry. If desired, apply leaf antiquing glaze and let dry before finishing with a final coat of sealer.

materials

Solid construction and a charming curved front made this buffet cabinet, *this photo,* a keeper despite chips and scratches. A little wood filler and a few coats of paint helped mask the flaws. Sparkly glass drawer pulls and knobs and trendy patterned door fronts breathed new life into the traditional piece.

Paint pens make easy work of adding detailed designs to furniture.

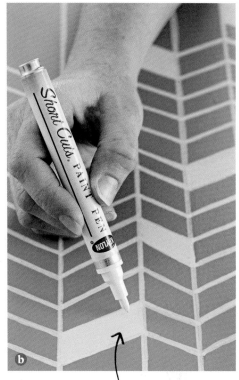

Herringbone Pattern

This drawn-on design is easy to achieve. The imperfect application is forgiving and doable for all skill levels.

materials

- Pencil
- Straightedge
- White paint pen
- Finish sealer

before

instructions

1 Remove painted cabinet doors and place on a protected surface. Use a pencil and straightedge to draw vertical lines along the door surface (*a*), varying the spacing between the lines.

2 Draw over the pencil lines using a white paint pen. When vertical lines are dry, use the paint pen to draw diagonal lines, alternating up and down between the vertical lines to create the herringbone pattern. When dry, give both the vertical and diagonal lines a second coat if needed to intensify the color.

3 Use the paint pen to randomly fill in sections between diagonal lines (*b*). Let dry and add a second coat. When dry, apply two coats of finish sealer.

You could add a few hits of random color to the design by using a second pen color.

before

Paper Mosaic

Don't let the tile look on this dining cart, *right,* fool you— this mosaic is fashioned from just paper and decoupage medium. Prime and paint the cart first and let dry. Sketch your design very lightly with pencil on the tabletop. Cut small pieces of paper in desired colors.

Starting with the flowers, use decoupage medium to secure pieces of paper to the cart. Be generous with the medium, and press to secure all edges of paper. Secure remaining pieces of paper, starting with the perimeter of the shape first and filling in the middle and around the flowers. When dry, coat the entire tabletop with the medium, pressing down any paper edges.

When dry, sand with fine-grit sandpaper, wipe with a tack cloth, and apply another coat of medium. Repeat three or four times or until you achieve the depth desired. **TIP:** *For added depth, select papers with mottled color and tone-on-tone designs.*

Doodle Design

This kitchen hutch, *left,* blooms with a dazzling bouquet treatment courtesy of bright-hue Sharpie markers. Because black Sharpie tends to bleed into lighter colors—especially yellow—draw the stems, leaves, and flowers first, then carefully fill in the petals and leaves with color. The key to this design is extending the stems over multiple surfaces.

Complete the look by using a metallic silver marker to draw a scale pattern on the back of the cabinet, starting in the upper left corner and working down and across. If you're worried about making mistakes, sketch your design in pencil first.

TIP: *When painting over Sharpie-marked furniture, first cover the area with a coat of oil-base primer.*

materials

Haute Hutch

Paint and wallpaper perk up an old display cabinet, **opposite**. Remove the door and shelves, then prime and paint it white. When dry, mask the raised details on the side panels and paint the panels creamy white. Let dry.

Following the manufacturer's instructions on a silver-leaf kit, apply adhesive to desired areas using a small detail brush. Here, the adhesive was painted in a thin line to accentuate the raised detail on the side panels, **right**, around the turned legs, and inside the recessed area along the cabinet's edge, **far right.** Let dry per instructions, then apply silver leaf to all adhesive areas, patting down using a paintbrush. Sweep away remaining loose bits of leaf using a soft paintbrush. Seal the leaf areas.

Cover the inside back with coordinating prepasted wallpaper, **right.**

before

More for Doors

Here are a few additional ways to mask glass-front cabinet doors.

Fabric Remove glass and mount fabric to glass front using spray adhesive, and then reinstall. Or place fabric behind the glass and tape to back of cabinet door.

Wallpaper Remove glass and mount prepasted paper to the front of the glass. Reinstall glass.

Window Film Remove glass and adhere window film or contact paper to the front. Reinstall glass.

Etching Cream Remove glass and apply etching cream or spray per manufacturer's instructions. Reinstall glass.

Paint Remove glass and spray-paint the back. When dry, spray with a sealer to protect. Reinstall glass.

Revive a china cabinet with paint and new hardware, *this photo*. Remove doors and drawers, masking drawer boxes so that just the fronts are primed and painted. Painting the boxes may cause them to not fit properly. Prime and paint the rest of the cabinet, apply mirror paint to the glass panels, and add new knobs and pulls.

Mirror Glass

A weathered mirror treatment applied to glass cabinet doors adds a touch of vintage style and conceals contents behind the cabinet doors.

materials
- Krylon Looking Glass spray paint
- Spray bottle with 1:1 vinegar and water mix
- Clean cotton rag

instructions

1 Remove glass panels from cabinet doors and place them right side down on a protected work surface in a well-ventilated room. Spray the back of the glass with Looking Glass Paint according to instructions on the paint can (*a*). Five coats were used on these panels; let paint dry between each coat.

2 Spray the painted surface with the vinegar mixture as desired, blotting with a rag to remove small patches of the paint (*b*). Re-spray one coat of Looking Glass paint over the entire surface to complete the mottled finish. Let dry.

3 Before replacing painted glass panels, paint entire cabinet using semigloss latex paint in an antique white hue. Craft unique door pulls from vintage objects. For these pulls, **right,** water-spigot handles were glued to vintage doorknob backplates then painted turquoise. Costume-jewelry earrings (with clips removed) were glued to the center of the spigot handles.

before

Blue paint unifies mismatched vintage hardware.

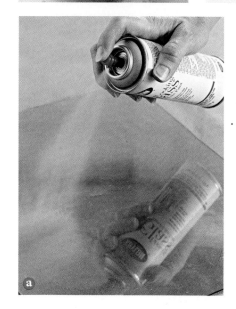

Bench Booster

A basic bench gains a load of character from shapely chair backs, *right*. Look for cast-off chairs—those with damaged seats or legs are just fine.

Cut the backs from the chairs. Measure and cut a piece of plywood to fit across the back of the bench, so when secured under the lip of the bench seat, it makes a flush surface for securing the chair backs, *below*. A 1×6 board worked for this bench, but you may need something thicker. Screw the board to the bench and the chair backs to the board. Paint entire piece and let dry.

Soften a wooden chair or bench with a purchased or easy-sew cushion.

tips & tricks

When looking for chair backs to fit your bench, be sure to measure the length of the bench and find backs to equal that length when set side by side.

Timeless Trim

A do-it-yourself nailhead accent gives plain furniture a high-end look without a high-end price tag. To accentuate the shape of this dining chair, *left*, high-dome nailheads were added along the back, bottom, and piped arm.

Select a chair with a firm frame to catch the nails as they are tapped in. Use needle-nose pliers to hold each nail as you tap it in place with a rubber mallet, *below*. Make sure spacing is uniform by measuring and marking placement for each nail, or by using a nailhead spacer tool as you work.

materials

gallery of great ideas

There are countless ways to reinvent dining chairs without a big investment.

Ideas to Spare

Explore even more techniques and treatments for kitchen and dining chairs.

Slipcover Purchase a ready-made slipcover, or if you can't find one to fit, make an easy-sew slipcover.

Decal Embellish chairs with vinyl decal designs.

Photo Transfer Use photo-transfer medium or water-slide decal paper to transfer photos onto furniture.

Specialty Paints Experiment with specialty paint finishes such as crackle, hammered metal, metallic, stone, or glitter.

Paint Techniques Create various effects using decorative painting tools such as combs, patterned rollers, wood-grain tools, denim brushes, and more.

Yarn Bomb Cover a chair with knitted or crocheted pieces, or simply wrap it with braided or individual lengths of yarn.

Woodburning Use a woodburning pen to hand-draw designs onto wood chairs.

Create dimension by gluing chipboard shapes to the chair and then painting it, *above.* Find chipboard shapes at crafts or scrapbooking stores, and use an all-purpose crafts glue to adhere them to the chair. The chipboard alphabet used here results in a unique, modern look.

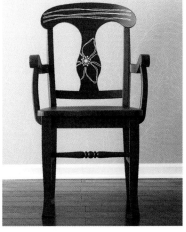

Use contrasting colors to make decorative accents pop. This chair, *above,* was painted white. When dry, automotive striping tape was applied in lines across the top and in a flower design in the center before the chair was coated with red paint. When dry, the tape was removed to reveal the white designs underneath.

A classic paisley stencil looks modern when applied with black paint on a white slipcover, *above.* To achieve a free-flowing composition, place the stencil a little off-center, and carry it off the top and bottom edges of the chair. Use a pencil eraser to apply black dots to mimic the look of nailheads along the bottom edge.

Solid-back chairs work perfectly for this drilled-through design, *above.* Find or create a pattern composed of circles ranging from ¼ to 1 inch in diameter to match basic drill-bit sizes. Print and tape the paper pattern to the chairback. Drill through the circles using various drill bits.

Use paper to transform a chair, *above.* Remove the chair seat, and decoupage it using art paper or wrapping paper and decoupage medium. While drying, decoupage the frame of the chair, cutting paper into manageable sizes and overlapping when needed. When dry, replace the seat.

Let two tones of wood stain give a rich look to an unfinished chair, *above.* Apply a wood conditioner to the entire chair before staining. Follow stain instructions to apply the stain using a clean cotton cloth or brush, using a lighter stain color on the chairback and a darker color on the seat and frame.

Easy-Clean Covers

Spruce up tired kitchen chairs with oilcloth or laminated fabric, *inset photo*. Select chairs with seats that are easy to remove, *this photo*. Remove the seat and cut fabric large enough to wrap to the underside. Lay the fabric right side down and place the seat on top, also right side down. Pull fabric taut from the center of each side and staple to the seat. Continue to staple around entire seat. These chairs feature styles that allow fabric to be added to the chairbacks by wrapping and stapling fabric in a similar manner to covering the seats.

Experiment with other produce such as bok choy, oranges, apples, and peppers.

These hand-painted leaves add extra detail and help fill in and connect the design.

Veggie Stamping

No need to buy expensive flower stamps to achieve this custom-printed look. Just hit the grocery store for a fresh bunch of celery!

materials
- Celery bunch
- Knife and cutting board
- Masking tape
- Disposable plate
- Fabric paint
- 1-inch-wide foam brush
- Paper towels
- Style stick
- Iron and press cloth (optional)

instructions

1 To make the stamp, cut celery 2–3 inches from the end (*a*), then wrap tape around the end to hold the stalks together. Let dry for 20 minutes, as the fresh cut will produce moisture on the celery.

2 Pour paint onto a disposable plate, and use the foam brush to apply a thin layer of paint to the cut celery ends. Avoid dripping paint into the area between the stalks—it will cause the flower shape to be less defined.

3 Test the stamp by firmly pressing it onto a paper towel. Reload the stamp with paint and press onto the fabric-covered seat (*b*). Remove the stamp without sliding it. Repeat in your desired arrangement. Let dry.

4 Dip style stick into paint, roll off excess, and paint on leaves as desired (*c*). Let dry.

5 Heat-set if desired per paint instructions using an iron and press cloth.

Upgrade fabric seats with a quick and thrifty paint embellishment, *this photo*. Purchase rubber or foam paint stamps, or use celery to stamp flowers like on these kitchen chairs.

Island Style

A recipe for success, this multitasking island, *right,* caters to storage fanatics. The island was fashioned from two matching buffets secured back to back and painted teal. A quartz-surfacing countertop and casters finish the structure before it's decked out to store kitchen essentials.

For quick-grab paper towels, mount closet rod brackets inside an open cubby, *above,* and use a dowel to hold the towels in place. Wire racks, trays, and cutting boards might have to share a compartment, but tension rods divide and designate separate spaces for them, *above right.* Because the rods are movable, they can change as your collection does.

TIP: *Open cubbies and shelves mean supplies are right at hand, but they can also expose unsightly messes. Baskets keep items accessible yet concealed.*

Retrofit Table

Cook up more counter space by outfitting a basic kitchen worktable with storage accessories, *left*.

Before painting this table with a washed green treatment, the butcher-block top was masked. A wooden bin and cutting-board holder were painted to match. When dry, drawer glides were added to the bottom of the bin and to the table shelf to create an easy-access pullout drawer, *below left*.

A wine rack and wire drawer mounted under the tabletop house kitchen staples. The side of the table is also put to use holding a utensil cup and spice rack, *below right*.

Top It Off

If this concrete look doesn't appeal to you, try one of these other ideas for the surface of your island project.

Faux Granite Look for DIY products that promise a believable granite look.

Butcher Block Have a piece of butcher block cut to fit your island top.

Tile Cut a piece of plywood or MDF, then cover it with ceramic or granite tiles.

Laminate Find a prefabricated laminate top at a hardware store or home center.

MDF It's not fancy, but cutting a piece of MDF is inexpensive, and it can be painted and then topped with a food-safe sealer.

Repurposed Wood Recycle a solid-wood door or extra wood flooring as an island top.

Fashion the perfect kitchen island by piecing together two ready-made carts and a wine rack, adding false backs between and painting the entire assembly aqua blue. Casters and a on-trend concrete finish complete the makeover, *this photo*.

before

Concrete Surface

Give a basic countertop sleek, modern style with this concrete finish technique.

materials

- Plastic drop cloth
- MDF countertop
- Primer
- Safety glasses and face mask
- 5-gallon bucket
- Ardex Feather Finish in gray
- Electric drill and mixing attachment
- Putty knife
- Plastic scraper
- Electric sander or sanding block
- 60- and 220-grit sandpaper
- Damp cloth or shop vac
- Food-safe satin concrete sealer

instructions

1 Protect work surface and surrounding areas with plastic. Prime MDF countertop and let dry. Wearing safety glasses and a face mask and following package instructions, use a drill and mixing attachment to mix Feather Finish with water in a 5-gallon bucket to the consistency of toothpaste (*a, b*).

2 Using a putty knife, spread a thin layer of the mixture over the primed MDF (*c*), coating the top and all sides and spreading smooth. Use a plastic scraper to knock off the texture and smooth the surface further (*d*). Let dry 20 minutes, then smooth the edges with a damp finger. Let dry.

3 Sand the surface using 60-grit sandpaper (*e*). Wipe with a damp cloth or clean with a shop vac.

4 Repeat steps 2 and 3 four times. On the fourth sanding, use 220-grit sandpaper.

5 Apply five coats of concrete sealer using a clean cloth and following manufacturer's instructions (*f*). Let dry.

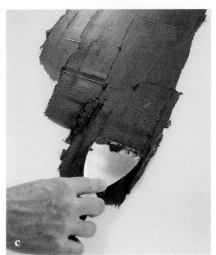

Relocated Dresser

Originally meant for the bedroom, this dresser, *left*, makes a fun and functional kitchen island. Before priming and painting the piece aqua blue, the bottom drawer and hardware were removed, and the stained top was masked.

For nontraditional drawer pulls, braided leather strips were attached using bolts and washers, *above*.

TIP: *When repurposing furniture for the kitchen, look for pieces that are close to standard 36-inch counter height. Often legs can be cut down to lower a piece or casters added to raise it.*

Reinvented Table

In another life, this piece was a hospital tray table, complete with unsightly brown veneer. After a thorough cleaning, the top was painted chartreuse green. When dry, it was masked with sticker paper cut into flower shapes and automotive striping tape formed as branches. Then it was painted white. When the paint was still tacky, the masks were removed to reveal the green design underneath, *this photo* and *inset photo*.

Achieve the look of exotic furnishings at a fraction of the cost.

Inlaid Look

This laminate-top table, *right* and *below*, had been kicked to the curb before it was rescued with a whole new look. The original plastic legs were replaced with stainless-steel ones, and the top was given a high-end bone-inlay treatment with nothing but paint, a stencil kit, and a few hours.

The top was first painted black. When dry, the center of the table was marked and the stencil-kit directions followed to apply bone-color paint over the stencils. When dry, a spray sealer was applied over top.

TIP: *Try using a sponge roller rather than a stencil brush to speed up the process.*

Use leftover scraps of ribbon to dress up a plain photo mat.

Ribbon Accents

Pink and yellow ribbons kick up the style of a wooden dining set, *left*. Choose solid and striped ribbons in the same color family, and then have fun adhering them to elements of the furniture you want to emphasize, such as the table and chair aprons.

To adhere the ribbons, use double-sided Sealah tape, following package instructions.

tips & tricks

When adding ribbons to furniture, remember less is more. If the piece calls for additional decoration, use paint or another technique to complement the ribbon treatment.

Tape Stripes

Completing this pop-modern look is an easy and inexpensive way to achieve a bold design. Best of all, it's not permanent!

materials

- Paintbrush
- Primer
- White paint
- Washi tape in desired colors
- Crafts knife and sharp blade
- Metal ruler

instructions

1 On a protected work surface, prime (***a***) and paint the table, letting dry between coats.

2 When dry, apply washi tape in desired design. For this table, the vertical stripes were applied first, carrying the striping over the top (***b***) in an off-center position that continues over the side of the table then down the legs.

3 To create a herringbone pattern, mark a center point for the design and lay strips of tape at a slight angle along each side. Allow ½-inch spacing between each strip. Overlap the tape slightly at the center point, and change colors as desired (***c***).

4 Trim the tape ends ¼ inch to the right of the center line using a sharp crafts knife and metal ruler. Slice through just the tape layer, using light pressure so you don't mar the tabletop (***d***). Repeat the cut ¼ inch to the left of the center, then peel away the small trimmed ends (***e***) to reveal your masterpiece (***f***).

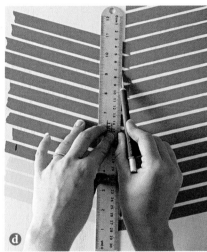

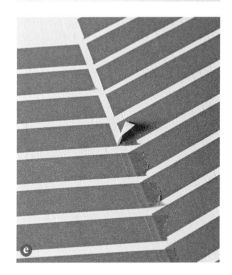

before

Colorful stripes on your dining table, *left*, might make you a little nervous at first, but the inexpensive tape stripes can be easily removed if you tire of the look. Prime and paint the unfinished table bright white. When dry, peel and stick to your heart's desire using washi tape or colored masking tape. Flip to *page 75* to see an entirely different way to make over this same table!

Washed Stain and Wood Carving

Create a one-of-a-kind table with an easy stain treatment and hand-carved accents.

materials

- White oil-base paint
- Turpentine
- Small containers for mixing
- Rags
- Wood stain in a dark color
- Wood chisel
- Clear sealer (optional)

instructions

1 Mix ½ cup white paint and ½ cup turpentine in a small container. That will be enough to cover a 38-inch-square tabletop. Rub mixture into table surface using a soft rag (*a*). The mixture soaks into the wood, leaving no wipe marks.

2 While the paint is still wet, wipe on the wood stain using a new soft rag. The white grain should show through (*b*). Because the stain is dark, you shouldn't need much.

3 When the stain is dry (wait at least 6 hours), use a sharp wood chisel to make vertical strokes in the surface to carve your design (*c*). Follow the wood grain when you make your strokes (going against the grain will splinter wood-veneer tables like this one). Keep the design shallow so food and debris don't get stuck in the grooves; carve just deep enough to reveal raw wood.

4 Rub a small amount of the thinned paint into the grooves (*d*), then wipe off excess. Repeat steps 3 and 4 to add your design to the table legs. Finish with a clear sealer if desired.

a

b

c

d

Two techniques result in a table makeover that's twice as nice, *left* and ***opposite***. The aged-driftwood finish was achieved by combing thinned white paint with stain. The rich color set the stage for large-scale rose designs—a doable wood carving project for DIYers.

before

tips & tricks

For this lustrous satin surface, choose oil-base paint rather than quick-drying latex. Oil-base paint applies smoothly and pairs well with stain. The finish will be worth the extra cleanup.

Try cutting cork tiles on the diagonal for even more design options.

For a fun centerpiece, float candles, flowers, and wine corks in a vase of water.

Cork Tabletop

Camouflage a damaged or drab tabletop with inexpensive cork floor tiles, *left*. Cork floor tiles are resilient, environmentally friendly, and low-maintenance. They have a rich, natural look and come in many colors and patterns.

Using ½-inch-thick cork floor tiles, plan a checkerboard pattern using a variety of tile patterns, or use the same pattern for a more unified look. Use a utility knife and a metal ruler to trim tiles with a clean, straight edge as needed. Adhere each tile to the wood surface with wood glue.

TIP: *Search home stores for other flooring materials to try on your tabletop, such as ceramic tiles or peel-and-stick vinyl floor tiles.*

Oversize Design

Welcome guests to your table with a universal sign of hospitality: a pineapple, *right*. In a reverse-stencil technique, paint the table ivory using flat latex paint. Then cut the pineapple pattern from adhesive shelf paper and stick it on. For graphic pop, place the pineapple off-center and let it carry over the table edges. Paint the table again using an orange hue. When almost dry, peel off the shelf paper to reveal the pineapple.

TIP: *Run a credit card or burnishing tool over the shelf paper to seal the edges tight to the table before painting.*

Give wood floors a makeover with durable floor paint and several coats of protective sealer.

If your spice container isn't magnetic, glue a magnet to the back.

Pantry Power

When outfitting a piece of furniture as a kitchen pantry, keep these tips and tricks in mind.

Depth Deeper cabinets aren't always better. A shallow cabinet means items don't get pushed to the back of a shelf and forgotten about.

Shelves Look for cabinets with several adjustable shelves so you can select the heights that work best for the items you store. Measure and mount shelves to accommodate your containers.

Grouping Use cabinet organizers to help group like items into zones (baking, snacks, tools, canned goods, etc.).

Labels Use labels on shelves or containers so family members return items to the right place.

Purge The best organizing tip for any pantry is to stay ahead of the mess by regularly clearing out stale items and tidying up everything else.

Kitchen Corral

If you need more kitchen storage, turn a freestanding cabinet or armoire into a hardworking pantry, *opposite*. Make use of the cabinet door backs by installing a sheet of cork to post recipes and notes, installing a sheet of galvanized metal to hold magnetic hooks and spice jars, *far right,* and painting one with chalkboard paint to keep little ones occupied.

On shelves and in drawers use a variety of organizers—plastic risers, lazy Susans, baskets, bins—to stow food and supplies, *right* and *below right*. Glass jars, *below, far right,* are especially nice because you can see what's inside. Labels identify contents.

tips & tricks

When transferring food from its original package to an airtight jar or a pretty basket, be sure to mark the new vessel with the product's expiration or freshness date as well.

For easy art, use plate hangers to hang a trio of colorful dishes.

before

Recycled Cabinet

Old entertainment cabinets are aplenty, collecting dust in thrift shops and basements everywhere. Repurpose a cabinet as a handy kitchen storage depot, *opposite*. Remove the unwanted doors and drawers, then sand, prime, and paint the unit. For a pot rack, *above, far right*, cut a sheet of hardboard pegboard large enough to cover the back opening, adding ¼ inch to all sides of the panel. Prime and paint the panel, and attach it to the back of the unit with screws, painted side facing forward. Hang pans and kitchen tools from S hooks.

Stow countertop appliances, baking molds, and cutting boards on open shelves, and tuck table linens into a pretty basket. Span an open space with a tension curtain rod to create a clever towel bar. Mount organizers on the side of the unit to keep supplies accessible, *above left*. Turn an exterior wall of the cabinet into a message board by painting it with chalkboard paint, *right*.

Craft a convenient organizer with 4-inch-diamater PVC pipe, *above middle*. Cut the pipe into desired lengths using a power chop saw or a miter box and handsaw. Prime and paint the pieces, then adhere them to the shelf using construction adhesive or screws.

Bedrooms & Bathrooms

Let reinvented furniture give *unique character* to your home's *personal spaces.* Whether you're primping for a new day or relaxing after a long one, *creative makeovers* give bedroom and bathroom furniture individual style.

Makeovers don't get much easier than this! To make a spindle headboard even sweeter, sew ribbons to a colorful ticking-stripe rug, drape it over the headboard, and tie in place, *this photo*. The rug makes the piece appear more substantial and is easily removed to change the look.

Streamlined Storage

A budget-conscious facelift for a 1960s hutch yields sophisticated style and smart storage in a small bathroom, *right*. A back panel was added then the piece was updated with chic cream and coral paint and brushed-brass hardware. Its tall, slim profile maximizes wall space without eating up floor space. Open shelves provide grab-and-go perches for towels and water-resistant woven totes filled with toiletries.

Look for cabinets with a depth of 21 inches or less so it doesn't extend beyond a standard vanity.

before

Overlay Accents

Give a boring vanity custom-crafted flair by gluing lightweight decorative fretwork overlays to the drawer fronts, *left* and *above.* Expanded-PVC-foam overlays are typically ⅛-inch thick and come in standard sizes that can be trimmed with a utility knife to fit drawer fronts or cabinet doors. For a more custom look, order the fretwork panels in your desired sizes and thicknesses. To install, brush clear silicone adhesive on the back of the overlay and press in place. The white overlays can be painted with spray paint suitable for plastic, or a primer for plastic topped with latex paint.

TIP: *This monochromatic scheme has a sophisticated vibe, but if you want the fretwork to stand out, paint the pieces a contrasting hue before applying them.*

Vintage Vanity

Before painting this sideboard a soothing aqua hue, *left*, a hole saw was used to drill through the top to accommodate two sinks. The stained top was then finished with a clear marine varnish to protect it from water. When dry, the top was masked, hardware removed, and the base was painted inside and out. To create accessible open shelving, and to showcase pretty towels and containers, the two center drawers were removed (and reused on the walls), *opposite*.

Dated metal cabinet knobs were replaced with easy DIY knobs, *above*. To make these dahlia-motif knobs, start with plain white porcelain knobs 1½–2 inches in diameter. Use a Sharpie marker to draw on the design, and let dry for 24 hours. Place the knobs on a cookie sheet and bake at 350°F for 30 minutes to set the paint. The paint color may change slightly after baking, so test colors first if desired.

tips & tricks

When searching for unique vanity cabinets, know that standard height is 32 inches. But depending on your height, you might want to go as high as 36 inches.

before

Surface-mount sinks make it easy to convert a dining room sideboard into a double-sink vanity for a master bath, *this photo.* Outfit the piece inside and out with storage-savvy accessories.

Drawers removed from the sideboard make a pair of unique mirrors with built-in shelves.

hair care

Retrofit Sink

If you're looking for an alternative to ordinary cabinets but don't want to pay top dollar for a unique furniture-style vanity, turn a vintage buffet or dresser into a sink vanity, *right*. You may lose use of all or some of the top drawers, but ample counter space and makeover bragging rights make up for it.

Find a piece that is deep enough to accommodate your sink and faucet fixtures. You can save a little space by using a wall-mount faucet or a surface-mount sink. For instructions on converting a buffet into a sink vanity, see *page 188*.

Reproduction vinyl ceiling tiles were cut to fit the recessed door panels on this cabinet, and a swing-arm towel bar was mounted inconspicuously to the side, *below*.

Make a medicine cabinet by crafting a box with shelves and hinging to framed mirror.

From storage to seating, makeover projects boost bathroom spaces in no time.

Mix and Match

Three charming pieces were creatively combined to create a one-of-a-kind station for storage and getting ready, *above*. The top part was originally a kitchen cupboard missing its base, and the bottom part was a bedroom vanity without a mirror. The seat was a sewing stool.

To help unite the pieces, new matching glass knobs replaced the old hardware. A blue-and-white color scheme with paint, fabric, and wallpaper further joined the unlikely trio to form a functional and charming bathroom ensemble.

TIP: *If storage is a priority, look for a seat that opens to reveal storage inside. A pretty skirt conceals the storage box on this sewing stool.*

Renewed Bamboo

The damaged finish on this old cane-back bamboo chair, *above*, was vanquished to show off its delightful silhouette and petite frame, perfect for a small bathroom space. For a bright sheen, the chair was spray-painted using a glossy latex paint in vibrant red to contrast with the mostly white bathroom.

For the seat, a new cushion was fashioned from fabric in a modern chevron pattern. To accent the chair back, narrow grosgrain ribbon was woven through the caning using a criss-cross pattern to form asterisk-like motifs.

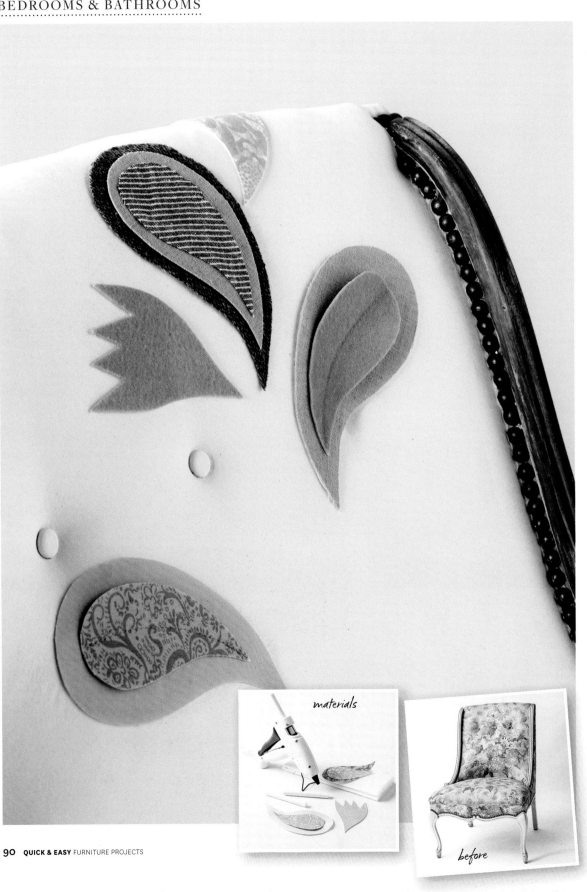

materials

before

Restyled Chair

This chair's redeeming qualities—a sturdy frame and nailhead trim, **opposite**—made it makeover-worthy. First priority was to do something about the unsightly floral fabric. Rather than reupholster the chair, the frame of the chair (including the nailhead trim) was masked with painter's tape, and the fabric was painted using two coats of white Chalk Paint. The paint glides on best if you dampen the fabric before painting it.

When dry, the painted fabric was masked (including the nailhead trim) and the frame was painted with one coat of gray Chalk Paint. When dry, a driftwood look was achieved by dry-brushing a small amount of white Chalk Paint on top and wiping away the excess with a clean rag. If desired, sand the wood lightly so some of the original stain peeks through.

To create the appliqués, cut three different sizes of the same shapes from fabric—in this case, three sizes of paisley shapes and one modern tulip shape, **left**. Apply no-fray liquid to all edges. Layer sets of the shapes, then sew them together with a single line of stitching through the centers so the edges on the top layers can pull up to show dimension. Attach the pieces to the chair using fabric glue sticks and a hot-glue gun, creating an asymmetrical design running down the front of the chair.

Chalk Paint

Not to be confused with chalkboard paint, Chalk Paint is a brand of decorative paint perfect for a variety of furniture makeovers. Here's why:

Easy to Use Chalk Paint rarely requires surface preparation such as sanding and priming.

Versatile Apply the paint to just about any surface, including wood, metal, and stone. It even works well on high-traffic surfaces such as floors, and it's suitable for both indoors and outdoors.

Eco-Friendly Chalk Paint is formulated with low volatile organic compounds (VOCs) and has no odor.

Consistency It has a thick, luxurious consistency that can be watered down to use as a color wash or exposed to air to thicken for an impasto technique.

Finish The finish is naturally matte, but a wax coat is recommended over top, which can be buffed to a satin sheen. For a glossier finish, top with polyurethane or polycrylic.

Stunning yellow paint and wood appliqués give a side table a whole new look.

Flower Chair

Bold flowers turn solid-color upholstered furniture into a conversation piece, especially when you're the artist! Stencils and acrylic paint mixed with textile medium were used to update this chair, *left*. Combine the paint and medium according to manufacturer's instructions, and stir the mixture thoroughly.

Determine flower placement, balancing sizes and color, and practice painting on scrap fabric first. Attach stencils one at a time using stencil spray adhesive. To achieve a thin layer, use a foam roller to paint from the outside of the stencil in. Then use a stencil brush for details.

When dry, mask the fabric and paint the chair frame a coordinating color.

TIP: *If you love this look but can't bring yourself to paint upholstery, drape your piece with a slipcover and paint that instead.*

tips & tricks

Before painting fabric upholstery, get the fabric slightly wet using a damp cloth or spray bottle of water. This allows the paint to adhere well by soaking into the fabric.

gallery of great ideas
Reimagine your bedroom furniture with these creative ideas and techniques.

Hide dated or damaged upholstery by covering it with new fabric, *above.* A cotton linen fabric was sewn into a pleated-skirt slipcover for the seat. For the back, a piece of the same fabric was cut to fit, stenciled with a monogram, and secured with glue around the edges of the old fabric. Matching trim hides the fabric's raw edges.

Citrus hues give this highboy a fun color-block transformation, *above.* Select a semigloss paint color for each drawer and a darker shade of one of those colors for the frame. Use sample-size pots of paint to save money. New porcelain knobs flaunt coordinating flourishes drawn on with Sharpie marker.

Linen-look wallpaper gives this piece a timeless look, *above.* The paper was applied to the top, sides, and drawer fronts, but the dresser's stained edges remain uncovered to frame the piece nicely. This wallpaper is vinyl-free and peels off easily, making the project fun for now and easy to change later.

Add an elegant touch to a wooden headboard by stenciling a cherry-blossom motif, *above.* To add dimension with shadowing and highlights, lightly dab a darker shade of the stencil color along one inside edge of the stencil and a lighter shade along the opposite inside edge.

For subtle pattern, stencil a drawer front using a tone-on-tone color scheme, *above.* The honeycomb pattern adds a playful touch to this small dresser without being too juvenile. Don't be afraid to try a bold color like hot pink or chartreuse to punch up a bedroom.

Wallpaper is an easy way to add personal style to furniture with little effort. A modern floral wallpaper rejuvenates this tired dresser, *above.* Paint the piece first, then apply coordinating wallpaper to drawer and door fronts, or even the dresser top.

A midcentury dresser gets a new, sophisticated style with two tones of gray paint, new drawer pulls, and a faux-granite top. Remove the drawers, lightly sand all surfaces, then wipe with a tack cloth before priming then painting.

before

materials

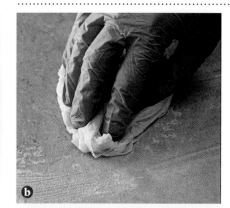

a

b

Granite-Look Surface

Create a sleek and durable surface with this paint technique achieved using a decorative paint kit.

materials

- Rust-Oleum's Countertop Transformations kit in Charcoal
- Rubber gloves
- Safety glasses
- Dust mask
- Tack cloth
- Rags
- Roller trays
- Foam rollers

instructions

1 Put on gloves, eye protection, and a dust mask. Use the kit's diamond-embedded sanding block to sand the surface in circular motions (**a**); wipe clean with a tack cloth (**b**).

2 Pour adhesive base coat into a roller tray. Apply with a foam roller (**c**) to the surface, then use the spray bottle to apply wetting agent to the surface (**d**). Once the base coat is applied, you have a 20-minute window to apply the color chips.

3 Use the rotary chip dispenser to spread decorative chips evenly over the entire surface (**e**). Let dry at least 12 hours.

4 After the surface dries, use a dry rag to brush off loose chips. Then use the chip scraper to smooth edges and remove additional loose chips. Be careful not to gouge the surface. Working in circular patterns, use the diamond-embedded sanding block to further smooth the surface (**f**). Compare your surface to the included sample swatch. When it feels similar to the touch, you are done sanding. Remove dust. The surface will appear lighter than the final result. Don't worry, it will get darker and shinier after all steps are completed.

5 Wearing gloves and eye protection, pour the contents of the Part A activator into the Part B base (**g**). Mix with the stir stick for two minutes. Pour the blended mixture into a paint tray.

6 Use a high-density foam roller to apply a heavy, even coat of the mixture to the surface (**h**). Once complete, roll a top coat onto the wet surface, rolling in one direction. Allow to dry undisturbed. It will be tack-free in four to six hours. Allow to cure for 48 hours before light use.

c

d

e

f

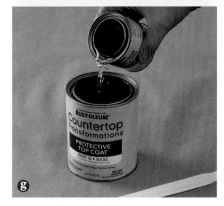

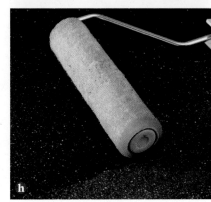

g

h

Faux Leather

Give a basic dresser this luxe, formal look, *left,* in just a few hours. Remove hardware and patch holes. Prime the dresser and let dry before painting with a satin-finish chocolate brown paint. The color on this dresser was matched to the leather drawer pulls, *above.* Be sure to paint drawer edges, too.

Add "stitches" to the frame, *top,* by drawing dashed lines using a gold-leaf pen and following a ruler to ensure they're straight. Repeat around the top and the drawers. Apply two coats of clear polyurethane, letting dry and sanding between coats. Measure and drill new holes for the drawer pulls and attach them.

TIP: *Use a damp cloth to wipe off any leaf-pen mistakes while the markings are still wet.*

Antique Finish

Milk paint and glaze give this new dresser vintage style, *right*. Remove hardware and patch holes. Add water to milk paint powder following manufacturer's instructions. Dry-brush paint onto dresser to create a scratchy crosshatch effect.

Paint molding strips white. When dry, use a miter saw to cut and miter the strips to fit outer edges of the drawer fronts. Attach with finish nails or wood glue. Apply antiquing glaze to the entire dresser, wiping off excess with a rag. When dry, coat the dresser with clear polyurethane. Measure and drill new holes for the drawer pulls and attach them.

materials

before

Stylized Flowers

A combination of stenciling and hand-painted touches gives this flower design a custom style.

materials

- Tack cloth
- Stencils
- Scissors
- Tape
- Stencil adhesive
- Stippling brush
- Semigloss enamel paint in three colors
- Paper plate
- Artist's brush
- Paint marker (optional)
- Polyurethane

instructions

1 Remove hardware and wipe the dresser clean with a tack cloth. Plan your design by arranging the stencils as desired to cascade across the top of the dresser and down the front. If needed, cut the stencils apart and tape off sections of the stencil you don't want to use.

2 Spray the back of the first stencil with stencil adhesive and place on the dresser. Dip the stipple brush into the paint (*a*) and dab off excess on a paper plate (*b*).

3 Apply light coats of paint using a pouncing motion with the brush perpendicular to the dresser (*c*). Repeat with the remaining stencils.

4 When dry, outline the images in the lightest paint color using an artist's brush (*d*) or a paint marker.

5 Finish by applying two coats of clear polyurethane, letting dry and sanding between coats.

before

a

b

c

d

Painted flowers perk up a tired dresser, *this photo and opposite.* The original hardware was removed and painted with a fresh and un-expected turquoise hue.

For easy artwork, insert wallpaper into a picture frame and layer it over an empty frame.

Kelly green turns a dated dresser into a showpiece, *this photo*. The dresser's charming curves made it impossible to pass up, but the damaged finish meant painting it was inevitable. With paint and new hardware, it now sings a contemporary tune.

Hand-Drawn Outline

A bold color choice sets this makeover in motion, resulting in a dramatic facelift for little investment. Remove drawers and prep all surfaces by lightly sanding and wiping them clean with a tack cloth. Prime the dresser and drawer fronts; let dry. Coat the dresser and drawer fronts with semigloss enamel paint. Two coats may be needed, letting dry between coats.

For the freehand outline, use a small artist's paintbrush dipped in white semigloss enamel paint, or try a white paint marker. A steady hand is a must, or you can follow a straightedge or apply painter's tape. Let the dresser's natural details be your guide. For this dresser, lines were applied to the curved top, *right,* drawer fronts, *below right,* raised accents on the sides, ball feet, and that irresistible apron, *below.*

TIP: *When painting a dresser with like-size drawers, be sure to number them when you remove them for painting. Drawers don't always fit perfectly in every opening, even if the drawers are the same size.*

tips & tricks

Hardware can change the entire style of a piece of furniture. From low-profile to attention-grabbing, modern to traditional, try a few options before committing.

Color Cues

Keep color psychology in mind to know what your choices are saying.

Blues Calming, reflective, tranquil, and cool. Evoke peace and sincerity.

Greens Reassuring and healing. Represent nature, life, and growth.

Reds Vibrant, exciting, and daring. Suggest power, energy, and passion.

Yellows Warm, optimistic, and cheerful. Signify happiness, joy, and intelligence.

Pinks Sweet, feminine, and fresh. Evoke compassion and faithfulness.

Purples Rich, luxurious, and spiritual. Denote wisdom, royalty, and dignity.

Oranges Stimulating, dynamic, and fun. Signify energy and vibrance.

Neutrals Reliable, versatile, chic, and restful. Suggest security and maturity.

Whites Fresh, pristine, and airy. Represent hope, simplicity, and purity.

Blacks Elegant, formal, and sophisticated. Suggest power and prestige.

Peel-and-Stick Wallpaper

If you like the look of wallpaper but not the mess of paste, this peel-and-stick project, *left,* might be for you. Prime and paint the headboard and allow it to dry. Use kraft paper to make a template of the areas you want to wallpaper. Lay the paper over the headboard, and etch the outline using a crayon or pencil. Cut out the pattern and trace it on the peel-and-stick wallpaper, then cut out.

Follow the manufacturer's instructions to apply the wallpaper, peeling it from the backing and pressing to the headboard surface. Use a burnishing tool to remove air bubbles. Because the wallpaper is repositionable, it's easy to remove and replace as needed. The bird stickers, *below,* are separate shapes that can be peeled from their backing and stuck to the wallpaper wherever you desire.

materials

Restyled Door

Two paneled doors from a salvage shop make this headboard project, *right,* affordable. A stencil in each recessed panel, *below,* offered subtle design and color while preserving the doors' rich wood finish.

Purchase a stencil or repurpose a plastic place mat with a pretty die-cut design, as was done here. Spray stencil adhesive on the back of the mat, and use a foam spouncer to apply pearlized acrylic crafts paint over top. When dry, fill in select areas with accent colors using a small artist's brush.

TIP: *Look for die-cut rubber or plastic place mats at discount or dollar stores. Paper, crocheted, or fabric doilies also make nice stencils.*

A vintage headboard and cast-off storage trunk, *this photo,* boasted charming lines but were in desperate need of fresh faces. Bold wallpaper and a painted pattern turned the drab pieces to fab in no time.

before

materials

Wallpapered Surface

With turned posts flanking a shapely headboard, this old piece, **above,** was too sweet to pass up. Because the height of the posts seemed a bit dated, they were cut down about a foot and treated to a fresh coat of white paint. The shorter posts were then topped with new wood finials, which were actually made for curtain rods. You could use vintage doorknobs to top the posts instead.

Wallpaper paste was applied to the headboard and the wallpaper placed on top, centering the pattern and letting the paper run a few inches beyond the edges of the headboard. A flexible plastic wallpaper smoother was used to remove any air bubbles. When dry, a sharp utility knife was used to trim the wallpaper around the edges of the headboard.

TIP: *If your headboard has beveled edges rather than flat ones, you'll need to cut the wallpaper to fit before adhering it.*

Patterned Roller

A pretty paint treatment was all it took to transform this dingy trunk, **above,** and emphasize its delightful details. Paint the trunk your desired color. When dry, use a patterned paint-roller set to roll on a design. Mix the base coat with a little white paint to create a lighter shade. Pour the color into a paint tray and follow paint-roller instructions to coat the roller with paint. Apply the pattern to the top and sides of the trunk.

Whether you're working with tone-on-tone hues like on this trunk or using colors with more contrast, test your color combinations on paper before applying them to the trunk.

TIP: *Use a flat or satin base coat so the roller isn't prone to slipping as it might with a semigloss base.*

Add blooms to a
headboard, *this photo* and
opposite, with a drill and
needle. Paint the headboard
white and let dry. Print
designs on paper, then
shade the back of the paper
with a pencil. Place the
paper on the headboard,
right side up, and trace the
design firmly, transferring
it to the headboard. Trace
the pencil lines with a
permanent marker, then
use a drill to drill holes
(a $5/32$ drill bit should
accommodate most yarns)
as desired along the design,
using the illustrations,
opposite, to help determine
hole placement for each
stitch. Use a darning needle
and yarn to fill in the design
with a mix of stitch styles.

before

Embroidery Stitches

With a needle in hand, you can accomplish all sorts of projects using these six splendidly simple stitches.

materials

- Embroidery floss or yarn
- Darning needle

instructions

1 Thread needle and knot one end. Used to create a solid outline, the backstitch is an easy go-to stitch. Working right to left, bring the needle up through the back of the project and create a forward stitch. For subsequent stitches, insert the needle a stitch length ahead on the back of the project, and bring the needle up and back to complete the stitch.

2 To make a basic running stitch, which is perfect for dashed outlines, pass the needle in and out of the project. Make the top stitch slightly longer than the underside stitches, and keep the stitch length uniform.

3 Add height and detail to projects with a French knot. Bring the needle through the back of the project to the front. Wrap the thread around the needle three or four times, keeping a tight grip on the thread. Push the needle down through the project just next to where it came out, holding the thread tight. Pull the needle through the knot to the back of the material.

4 For outlines with extra detail and thickness, use a stem stitch. Working the stitch left to right, bring the needle up through the back of the project on the pattern outline. Hold the yarn or thread toward you and make a short slanting stitch to the right. Continue stitching to complete the pattern.

5 Create quick leaves and petals with the lazy daisy stitch. Insert the needle on the back of the project, then pull the needle to the front. Insert the needle next to the first stitch, looping the thread under the needle. Pull the needle through to create a loop. Tie down the outside of the chain with a quick stitch, then bring the needle back up in position for the next stitch

6 Fill in designs using a long and short stitch. For the first row, use a backstitch to create alternate long and short stitches, following the shape of your outline. Keep working the following rows of stitches, keeping them the same length for a uniform look or alternating lengths for freeform style.

tips & tricks

For a similar look without drilling through furniture, embroider designs on fabric panels and use spray adhesive to secure them to the wood.

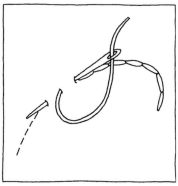

❶ backstitch

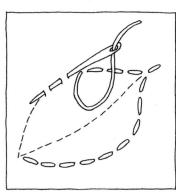

❷ running stitch

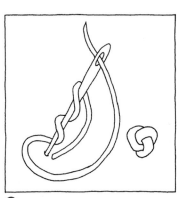

❸ French knot

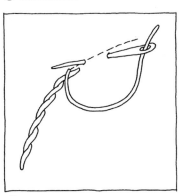

❹ stem stitch

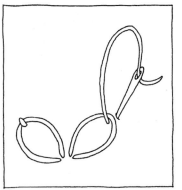

❺ lazy daisy stitch

❻ long and short stitch

Construct a storage headboard by grouping together discarded dresser drawers.

before

Pet Bed

A 1970s side table doesn't appeal to many, but this quick change to a pet bed, **right,** gives it a whole new purpose.

Remove the cabinet doors, clean the piece thoroughly, and patch hinge holes with wood filler. Sand all surfaces lightly and wipe with a tack cloth. Attach wooden furniture feet to bring the cabinet to a comfortable bedside-table height.

Prime, and then paint the cabinet with semigloss latex paint, letting dry between coats. When dry, insert a dog bed and any toys or treats to introduce your pet to the new space.

TIP: *To enclose the front but still make it pet-accessible, you could hang simple café curtains from a tension rod inside the cabinet.*

Paint Chip Tabletop

For a thrifty yet custom-crafted look, top a basic side table with colorful paint chips, *above.* Use scissors or a rotary paper trimmer to cut paint chips into uniform-size strips, *inset.* Arrange the strips on the tabletop as desired, and snap a photo of the arrangement before laying each strip facedown inside a cardboard box.

Spray the back of the strips with spray adhesive, and apply them to the tabletop one by one until the pattern is complete. Let dry, and then trim excess paper from the table edges using a crafts knife. Seal the top with two or three coats of glossy clear polycrylic spray. For extra protection, top the table with a piece of glass cut to fit.

TIP: *Before picking up paint chips, be sure to measure your furniture and determine the project's colors and basic configuration so you know which and how many chips to grab.*

Mirrored Drawers

Inspired by 1920s glamour, this fresh take on classic mirrored furniture, *above,* is sure to be a standout in your bedroom. Try this do-it-yourself approach as an inexpensive alternative to high-end mirrored pieces.

Paint a thrift store dresser white. Have mirrors cut to fit the drawer fronts. Most hardware stores carry mirrors and may be able to cut them to size for you. Pay extra to have the edges polished, especially if your drawers don't have recessed panels for the mirrors to fit inside.

Lay the mirrors facedown on a piece of plywood. Measure and mark locations for knobs. Drill through the markings using a diamond drill bit, holding the drill at a 90-degree angle. Drill at a constant speed with light pressure, and apply water to the area to keep the drill from overheating. Wear safety glasses and a face mask to prevent inhaling glass dust. Wipe dust away with a damp cloth. Attach mirrors to drawers using mirror mastic. When dry, carefully drill through the front of the holes and through the wood drawer fronts; install glass knobs, *inset.*

Stacked Tables

Take a bedside table to the next level by constructing a tiered table, *left*. One low side table with an integrated riser was used to make the keen tower.

The table was cut in two at the riser, leaving a longer end without a riser and a shorter end with the riser. All pieces were painted a fresh coral hue. When dry, the longer end was secured to the wall beside the bed using a French cleat, and the shorter end with the riser was placed on top and secured to the wall as well. A wood plant trolley, *below,* was painted to match and tucked underneath to make a fourth layer of storage that's easy to maneuver.

TIP: *If you can't find a table just like this to deconstruct, look for small stools or benches that would work.*

before

Marble Effect

Create a marbled look, *left,* using easy-to-do and inexpensive decoupage. Remove the drawer and doors. Paint the furniture casing and let dry. Use kraft paper to make patterns of the dresser top, drawer front, and doors. Trace the patterns on decorative paper and cut out. The paper chosen for this makeover mimics free-flowing marbled agate stone.

Apply thin, even coats of decoupage medium to the dresser top, and then gently place the paper on top, smoothing out trapped air bubbles with a squeegee. Repeat to add paper to the drawer and door fronts. When dry, seal the paper with a top coat of decoupage medium and let dry. Replace the drawer and doors, and add glass hardware.

TIP: *If you don't have a squeegee to smooth the paper, use a credit card.*

materials

If your walls aren't constructed of wood paneling like this, find wallpaper to mimic the look.

before

Multi-Crate Storage

Various-size crates take on a new task as bedside storage, *this photo.* Look for new or old crates in several sizes and with smooth, straight edges and sides. These crates were unified with a gray-wash technique on the exterior and painted bold colors on the interior. Then they were arranged like building blocks and screwed together to create a versatile mix of ledges and cubbies. Turning a couple of crates to one side means contents are concealed yet accessible from the bed. Climb the wall as high as you'd like, but you'll want to secure the crates to the wall.

Tape Accents

This little table, *right*, lacked style before it was rescued with fun washi tape and decorative masking tape.

The table was painted a soothing aqua hue and allowed to dry. Then strips of tape were applied to the sides and legs of the table to create horizontal and vertical stripes. On the tabletop, *inset*, flower shapes were made using small pieces of tape ripped from the spool to create raw edges. The taped designs are easily removed without damaging the painted surface.

TIP: *To make the designs permanent, coat the table with a clear sealer or decoupage medium.*

materials

before

before

Shoe Storage

With some reimagining, this boxy cabinet retained its storage power but claimed a fabulous new look, *left*. The door was removed and the existing shelves lowered to make way for custom shoe racks. To make the racks, screw ½-inch round dowels into the left side of the cabinet, then affix the dowels on the right side with an L-shape screw to eliminate holes showing on the outside of the cabinet. Repeat this process with a square dowel installed 2½ inches below and in front of each round one to give the toes of the shoes a place to rest.

The entire piece received a fresh coat of white paint, and the drawer fronts were highlighted with a soft shade of coral and finished with decorative knobs. A trio of hooks screwed to the outside of the piece adds quick-grab access for scarves or other accessories.

With a little TLC, storage pieces can flaunt both function and fabulous style.

A chevron pattern made from veneered MDF creates a stunning accent wall.

Trunk Refresh

Paint and fabric give this tired trunk a dashing new face, *left*. The trunk's exterior was first painted with hammered-silver spray paint and allowed to dry.

The edging and front hardware were masked off using painter's tape, and the front was painted a dark turquoise. When dry, a lighter turquoise paint was used to hand-paint a fun faux bois treatment. If you don't care to freehand the design, a wood-graining tool would create a similar effect.

The boxed cushion was sewn from linen fabric and contrasting turquoise piping to fit the top.

tips & tricks
Look for a trunk with a flat top rather than a camelback one, so the piece can function as bedroom seating as well as storage.

Use pretty wallpaper remnants to give old pieces fresh new looks.

Wall Cabinet Redo

A discarded display cabinet gained a new look inside and out with lipstick-pink paint and punchy damask wallpaper, **above**. The cabinet's straight, flat panels make this wallpaper project as easy as it gets. Simply measure and cut wallpaper to fit the cabinet door fronts, door backs, and inside back. Remove knobs and shelves and adhere each piece of wallpaper to the cabinet using wallpaper adhesive and following the directions on the container; let dry.

Install new knobs on the door fronts and pretty hooks on the door backs to hang necklaces. For smaller jewelry such as bracelets and earrings, use small cup hooks screwed to the underside of the bottom shelf.

Floor Screen Facelift

This privacy screen, **above,** had received three prior makeovers, but with 1980s ivy trellis fabric shirred onto rods inside each panel, it was ready for a fourth! The fabric and rods were removed and the frame was given a fresh coat of semigloss white paint.

Plywood panels were cut to fit inside each frame and wallpapered on both sides, then the panels were secured to the back of each frame. Now the piece stands tall and proud with this quick, affordable update.

TIP: *Wallpaper adhesive is surprisingly forgiving, so you'll have about an hour to reposition paper before the glue sets.*

Well-Dressed Wardrobe

Trick out a basic armoire as ultimate bedroom storage. This cabinet, *left*, was originally filled top to bottom with adjustable shelves. The top shelves were removed, and the highest of the remaining shelves was secured as a stationary shelf to help support a new vertical panel. This panel divides the top section to hold hanging clothes on one side and various storage containers on the other. Stray drawers just the right size were painted, labeled, and mounted to drawer glides on top of the two lower shelves.

A knob holding a mirror and a DIY jewelry holder make use of the cabinet door backs. Make a jewelry holder by securing decorative wire mesh to the back of a picture frame, and use small S-hooks to hold accessories.

TIP: *If you can't find a frame to fit your cabinet door, make one by gluing canvas stretchers together, painting them, and adding painted wood appliqués at the corners.*

Who needs a closet when you have a large cupboard like this? To prevent shelves from warping, use a center support and turn the shelves once a year. Or if they're too bad to salvage, replace them with MDF boards painted with an aged finish.

Country Chic Closet

Though freestanding cupboards aren't often needed in today's kitchens, they make charming storage pieces elsewhere. The dark walnut finish on this cabinet, *opposite*, was painted over using a flat sage hue and then given a weathered finish. To achieve the look, don't prime the piece before painting it; when the paint is dry, use fine-grit sandpaper to lightly sand away the paint so bits of wood show through, *above*. Wallpaper was applied to the inside back to lighten the interior.

Boost the cupboard's storage factor by retrofitting it with knobs and hooks to hold jewelry and other accessories inside and out, *above middle* and *right*, and using unexpected drawer organizers like this vintage muffin tin, *right*.

Mirrors cut to fit the door backs make this piece a perfect primping spot in the bedroom.

TIP: *Line old shelves with contact paper so the rough wood doesn't snag clothes.*

materials

Work Spaces

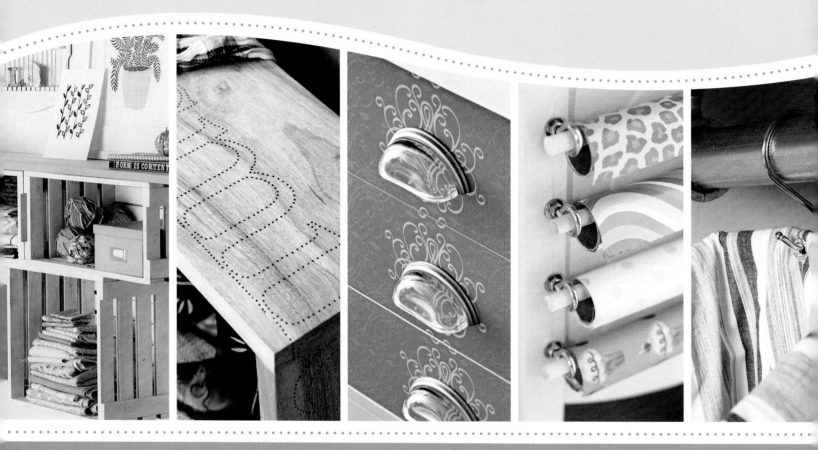

From mudrooms to home offices, *hardworking spaces* aren't always the most interesting ones. Turn the tables and lend unique, *personal style* to these areas with inspiring furniture projects you can do in a day and *on a dime*!

Roomy and versatile, a movable office, *this photo,* provides plenty of storage and desktop space. Use metal L-brackets to attach a wood countertop to two rolling drawer units, allowing enough room for seating in between.

Make a memo board by adding pegboard and cork panels to a trio of frames hinged together.

Rethink vintage finds and castoffs to create original organizers, *this photo,* capable of corralling all sorts of crafty things. Whether it's a desk, storage bins, or a memo board you need, be inspired to reuse and recycle furniture and accessories to reduce waste and reduce your costs.

Dresser into Desk

With paint and a few other modifications, this boxy midcentury-style dresser reveals a softer side and works wonders in a hobby space, *opposite.* A new top replaces the original, damaged one and features a 12-inch overhang on the back side to expand the work surface and accommodate seating.

Small wooden sewing drawers, *right,* and storage boxes replace the top drawers so supplies are quick to grab and take elsewhere. Easy-make labels, *below, far right,* identify contents and ensure everything is returned to the proper place. These are adhered with washi tape, but you could use sticker paper.

A new base cut from MDF and painted white, *below middle,* replaces the original peg-style feet to add a charming silhouette and raise the top to a comfortable 30-inch desk height. A common flea market find, a vintage tool caddy makes ideal desktop storage, *below.* Add a stencil or other paint accents to personalize the piece. With their divided compartments, wooden or metal toolboxes or caddies can help organize a multitude of craft and office essentials.

TIP: *If cutting a custom cabinet base isn't for you, look for wooden furniture feet, available in a variety of heights and styles.*

before

tips & tricks

When removing drawers to make way for more clever bins, boxes, or other containers, be sure to measure the drawer openings so you know what will fit.

Metallic Touches

Rich blue paint and floral fabric make a dramatic difference to a chair and desk, but it's the glamorous gold touches that provide their wow factor. To give the desk a fresh look, remove the drawers and hardware and mask the stained desktop. Paint the desk base high-gloss blue. Paint the drawer fronts a matte sheen of the same blue. When dry, use metallic gold crafts paint and a patterned paint roller to add interest to the drawer fronts. Follow the roller instructions and practice on paper first. Apply a clear sealer over the drawer fronts when dry. As a final bit of sparkle, install new gold knobs, **right,** and give the feet a dipped-paint look by masking them with tape and painting gold below.

To reupholster the chair, cut fabric and quilt batting to fit around the seat and chair back plus 3 inches all around. Remove the seat and back from the chair. Spray the back of the batting with upholstery spray adhesive and press on the seat, smoothing out wrinkles and wrapping to the underside of the seat; secure using a staple gun. Repeat to wrap batting around the chair back. Follow the same steps to wrap the seat and chair back with fabric.

To paint the chair gold, **below,** mask casters and other areas you don't want to paint. Spray the chair with primer suitable for metal. When dry, spray the chair with gold spray paint, and let dry before applying a protective clear coat. When dry, replace the newly upholstered seat and back.

TIP: *Patterned paint rollers are less prone to slipping around when applied over flat paint sheens. If you find some imperfections after applying the roller pattern, use an artist's brush to make touch-ups.*

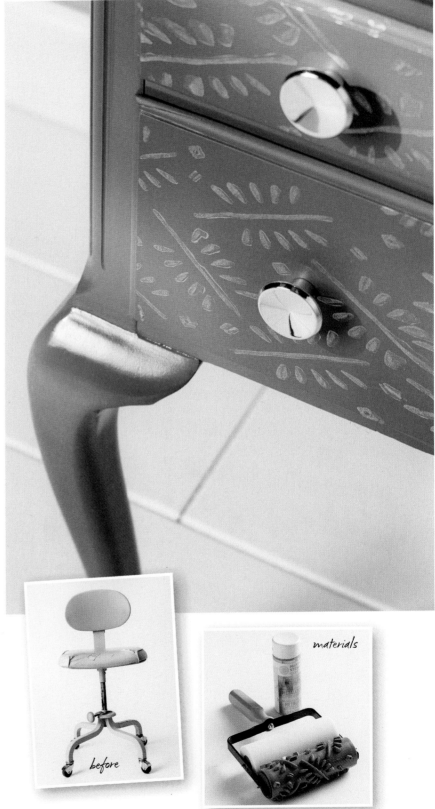

before

materials

A traditional Queen Anne writing desk and modern industrial chair, *this photo,* seem an unusual pair until a much-needed makeover joins them with a common color scheme and pretty patterns.

Relocated from the dining room, a large cabinet, *this photo*, works wonders as sewing room storage. The piece received cosmetic touches and a new top to better suit the space and its new duties.

Converted Console

Though it boasted a curvaceous apron and legs, the original black painted finish of this dining console didn't sit well when it was relocated to a cheerful hobby space. But after a few coats of chartreuse paint, the piece fit right in, ***top left***. A new MDF desktop was fashioned to extend nearly 18 inches past the cabinet back and painted with an oil-base white paint, which was allowed to cure for a week before installing.

Shapely furniture legs, ***top middle***, support the overhang on each corner. Wallpaper was applied to the console's door and drawer fronts, ***top right***, along with new glass knobs and pulls. All the special details give this space personal style. A glass food jar turns into a sweet pencil cup when a remnant of scrapbook paper is tucked inside, ***above left***. And the divided sections of this old chicken feed trough, ***above middle***, work well to organize colored stationery. Magnet labels are a must on its galvanized sides. A standard gray-and-black desk chair was certainly functional, but it begged to be covered with a stylish slipcover, ***above right***.

Office chairs are usually far from pretty, but a slipcover adds a soft decorative touch.

Marbled Desk

To give your work space a twist, try this colorful marbling technique, *right* and *above.* Pour 2 inches of water in a shallow container larger than each drawer. Pour a thin film of fingernail polish on top of the water (use new polish, as polish from opened bottles tends to congeal). This first layer of polish will coat the entire surface of the water. Drizzle on darker colors of polish, using a toothpick to combine the colors in organic swirls. Work quickly, as nail polish is designed to dry in minutes. Lightly dip a drawer front onto the polish mixture and lift straight up to remove. Place right side up to dry for at least 24 hours. Repeat for remaining drawers, pouring in fresh polish for each.

Let a marbling technique create functional artwork for your walls.

Refashioned Worktable

If you have a tight space that isn't suitable for a traditional desk, consider using a petite beverage or kitchen cart instead.

This cart, *left*, already had a drop-down panel on the side, but you could easily add a panel using a piano hinge and support bracket. Paint the cabinet to coordinate with your room, and add new hardware if desired. The original nickel knobs on this cart worked fine.

To maximize limited space, outfit the drawer with modular organizers, and corral supplies in a variety of pretty bins on the shelves. Cut a piece of cork to fit the door panel, and mount it on the back using spray adhesive. The side of the cabinet can be put to use with hooks or a magnetic strip.

TIP: *In lieu of cork on the door back, look for narrow storage bins made for cabinet doors.*

Maximize storage potential by utilizing panels on cabinet backs and doors.

Crafts Center

With new technology and low-profile televisions, large media cabinets are a thing of the past. When reinvented, however, the cabinets work wonders for stowing gobs of hobby supplies and make a thrifty alternative to pricey crafts or office furniture.

The boxy feet on this cabinet, *right,* were swapped out for feet with a softer profile, and then the original stained finish was painted blue with tan accents. Galvanized panels secured to the inside back and to one door back are loaded up with magnetic bins and containers, *below.* Shelves hold supplies neatly organized in baskets and binders. Ribbon embellishments on the front of each shelf were quick and easy to apply.

tips & tricks

To conceal contents on the shelves behind the glass door, you could cover the glass with wallpaper or easy-to-install contact paper or frosted film.

Office Armoire

No need to dedicate an entire room as home office space when you can contain it all in an armoire, *left.* These units can be placed in a guest room, the corner of a living room, or even in a wide hallway or entryway.

Depending on your decor, leave the unit stained or paint it to blend in.

For optimal desktop function, mount a piece of wood on drawer slides inside the cabinet. This surface can be pulled out when needed but tucked away behind closed doors when not.

To make use of vertical surfaces, thick cork panels were covered with a modern large-scale floral fabric. Cut cork to fit the cabinet back and door backs. Cut fabric 2–3 inches larger than the cork. Use spray adhesive to secure the fabric to the front, and then wrap fabric around all sides, pulling taut and securing to the back with spray adhesive. Hang the panels using removable adhesive mounting strips.

TIP: *Galvanized steel panels can also be cut and covered with fabric if you prefer to use magnets rather than pushpins.*

Entryway Organizers

A collection of wooden crates offers plenty of storage in a busy entryway, *right*. The versatile boxes are a manageable size and help sort belongings by season or family member. For two or more levels of stowing power, look for crates that can be easily stacked. Casters added to boxes on the bottom level make the whole stack mobile.

The fronts of these plain crates, *below,* were perked up with pretty wrapping paper remnants; sheets of decorative art papers or scrapbook papers would also work. Attach the paper using decoupage medium.

TIP: *Add a different color palette of papers to the back sides of the crates so you can turn them around for a whole new look.*

Drilled Bench

For this little project, *right,* you need only a drill, a design, and a wood surface. First, determine your design. Typography was used on this bench, *above,* but you might consider a geometric or organic shape. Print or photocopy the design onto paper, enlarging it to a size that fits your furniture. Tape the paper to the furniture. With a small bit, drill through the paper to make shallow, evenly spaced holes to outline your design. When done, remove the paper.

TIP: *Once you've determined how deep to drill each hole, mark the drill bit at that point by wrapping tape around it, which acts as your indicator to stop drilling.*

An unfinished bookcase flaunts delightful vintage charm courtesy of a whitewash treatment and classic stencil, *this photo.* By simply repositioning the shelves, the center portion opens up to accommodate coats and accessories, while the lower space is set up to stow a multitude of shoes and boots.

Bookcase Lockers

Use an unfinished bookcase to organize entry clutter. This tall, doublewide case, *opposite,* is freestanding, so it's much less expensive than custom, built-in cabinets.

To achieve a whitewashed finish, sand the case and wipe with a tack cloth, then stain a natural color. Mix white paint with glaze medium in a 1-to-1 ratio. Use a trim brush to apply the mixture to a section of the case, and then wipe with a damp lint-free cloth, removing most of the glaze. Continue in manageable sections until complete, and then stencil a design on the back panel in white paint. Apply a clear sealer if desired.

Carpet squares were cut to fit inside and stenciled with a playful shoe-tread motif, *above right.* A baking pan and pastry tins, *above, far right,* were repurposed as organizers for keys, spare change, and other small items. Numbered hooks, *right,* continue the vintage theme, and baskets with wipe-off tile labels, *far right,* neatly contain seasonal items on the top shelf.

tips & tricks
Rather than installing shoe shelves with uniform spacing, measure all footwear first and space the shelves to accommodate the various heights.

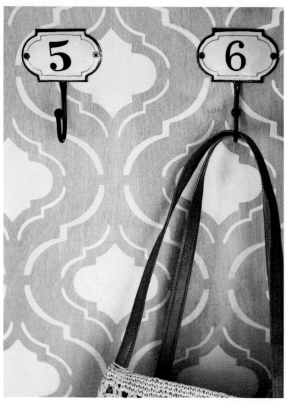

Choose an entry seat with storage potential over a standard boot bench.

Transformed Trunk

A diamond in the rough, this 1970s trunk, *above,* came complete with a ripped vinyl top and rusty casters, but also with ample space for seating and interior storage.

The old top was removed and reupholstered with a durable and stain-resistant indoor-outdoor fabric. The casters were removed, and wooden dividers were cut to fit inside, creating separate compartments for organizing shoes, hats, scarves, and other accessories.

Then the trunk received primer and two coats of white paint inside and out. New casters were installed to bring the trunk to a comfortable seating height.

The small side table was relocated from a bedroom and outfitted with a divider and power strip to create a convenient charging station at the back door.

TIP: *When adding casters to furniture, look for rubber casters that won't damage floors.*

Easy-to-install beaded board adds architecture to an entryway.

Creative Cubby

A bookcase designed to stand vertically, *left*, works even better on its side! The sturdy case was flipped horizontally and outfitted with casters and a custom-made cushion to become a modern entry bench with convenient storage cubbies.

As an alternative to sewing a cushion, you could line up several individual seat cushions on top of the piece. **TIP:** *For comfortable seating, be sure the height of your bench, including a cushion and casters or feet, is 18–20 inches.*

Refinished Drop-Leaf Table

Give a plain-Jane table more presence with a modern, chic stain-and-stencil makeover.

materials

- Stripper
- Paintbrush
- Putty knife
- Sandpaper
- Tack cloth
- Lint-free cloths
- Wood conditioner
- Stain
- White crafts paint
- Disposable plate
- Stencil
- Stencil adhesive spray
- Large pouncer stencil brush
- 2- to 3-inch chip brush
- Polyurethane

instructions

1 Follow manufacturer's instructions to strip the table, if needed, using paint and varnish remover (*a*), a paintbrush, a putty knife, and sandpaper.

2 After sanding and removing dust with a tack cloth, use a clean cloth to apply one coat of wood conditioner to the entire table according to the manufacturer's instructions.

3 Within 2 hours of applying the conditioner, stain the table with a cloth or paintbrush, stroking in the direction of the grain (*b*). Leave stain on for 5–15 minutes, then remove excess stain with a cloth. Dry 4–6 hours, then apply a second coat of stain, if desired. Allow to dry completely (about 8 hours).

4 Squeeze a small amount of paint onto a plate. With the table leaves up, spray the stencil back with spray adhesive and place on the table. Use the pouncer brush to apply a thin coat of the paint (*c*). Reposition the stencil as needed, matching the pattern using registration marks on stencil. Let dry.

5 Give the design an aged look by dipping a cloth into the stain and rubbing a small amount of stain on top of the design (*d*), then immediately wiping it off. Let dry.

6 To add dimension and a driftwood look to other areas of the table, use the chip brush to dry-brush them with white paint (*e*). Let dry, then seal with polyurethane (*f*).

Small tables are workhorses in the home, especially convertible styles like this drop-leaf entry table, *this photo.* The table's original pine finish gets a style boost with an allover gray stain and peacock-feather design stencil.

Staining Basics

Stain comes in many colors and forms—gels, liquids, and sprays. Keep these guidelines in mind.

Know your wood.
Hardwoods absorb stain more evenly. Paint-grade woods are lower-quality, and the grain may not be as appealing as better stain-grade woods.

Prep work pays off.
Properly prepping the wood before staining ensures a better end result. Sanding helps diminish dents and scratches, and it smooths out the surface so the stain application is more uniform.

Don't shake the can.
Shaking a can of stain creates unwanted air bubbles that transfer to the wood when the stain is applied. Instead, stir the stain to mix ingredients that have settled.

before

Tree Bark Embellishment

Inexpensive and easy to find, birch bark is a fun material to spruce up a plain cabinet, *right.*

Using heavy-duty scissors or a saw, cut sheets of dry birch bark into equal-size squares. Use contact cement to glue the pieces to cabinet door fronts in staggered rows. Fill empty spaces with more bark cut to fit.

TIP: *Birch bark can peel and chip in high-traffic areas. A clear sealer offers protection, but you will lose the natural finish.*

Small furnishings can be big helpers, adding storage or an extra place to sit.

Scour flea markets or salvage shops for cast-off shutters. These two 6-foot-tall shutters, *above,* were turned horizontally to form a large entry shelf. Three decorative shelf brackets were screwed to one shutter, and then the second shutter was screwed on top of the brackets. Six cast-iron coat hooks add the final layer of functionality.

A little fabric adds a load of style to a plain wooden chair, *above.* Remove the seat and back. Cover the seat with fabric, and secure with carpet tape underneath. Cover the seat back, spraying the fabric with adhesive, pressing it smooth to the wood, and securing with carpet tape at the back. Conceal the tape on the back by securing a piece of fabric with finished edges over top.

Imprinted with elegant typography and designs, wooden wine crates can double as stunning storage boxes, *above.* Inquire at liquor or wine stores for discarded crates; you should be able to get them for free or just a few dollars. Sand any rough areas, add casters, and you're done!

Reimagine a wall organizer as office storage. This kitchen plate rack, *above,* needs no modifications to transition into a work space, neatly dividing paperwork and notebooks above and corralling containers of supplies on a shelf and hooks below.

Don't settle for standard gray metal file cabinets. Paint them a bold hue! By pairing two cabinets together and topping with a solid-surfacing countertop, *above,* you create a storage cabinet nice enough to place anywhere it's needed.

The complementary colors on this bench, *above,* add vibrant contrast in a foyer. Paint the bench a lively orange hue and let dry. For a rustic finish, blue paint was dry-brushed over the orange. When dry, the raised panels were stenciled in orange. Finally, a clear sealer was applied.

Be open to bar-height desks so you have the option to stand to work.

Tutu Chair

Industrial design adds an eclectic touch to a modern or traditional space. This old lab chair, *right,* had the right construction but no cosmetic appeal. To hide the black vinyl, the chair was re-covered in a feminine floral print accented with pink piping.

The chairback was removed and reupholstered, adding two decorative button accents. A slipcover on the seat incorporates a bright aqua tutu as skirting. Check dance-supply companies or costume shops for large, colorful tutus. You may need to sew two together to fit around your chair.

Use a stainless-steel lab or restaurant worktable as a desk. Many have adjustable heights.

before

Midcentury Remake

Vivid blue vinyl cushions and a smooth white frame give this modern chair a new look, *left*. The cushions were removed from the chair, and then the fabric was removed to provide patterns for the new upholstery. The new vinyl covers were sewn with boxing strips and piping to fit the cushions.

The frame was sanded to remove the gloss sheen and give the wood a bit of tooth before it was primed and painted. When the paint was dry, the new cushions were reattached.

TIP: *For a brushstroke-free finish, use a paint sprayer rather than a paintbrush for your top coat.*

before

A pair of sawhorses and a custom top comprise this creative worktable, *this photo,* but it's the chair that steals the show. A plain white slipcover, *opposite,* was embellished with banding, a bow, and a painted monogram to make a throne-worthy seat.

Make thrifty magnet boards from old metal serving trays.

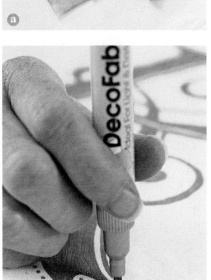

Slipcover Monogram

Transfer a monogram or other design to fabric with just a few steps and inexpensive supplies.

materials

- Design pattern
- Iron
- Cardboard
- Dressmaker's carbon paper
- Pencil
- Fabric paint marker

instructions

1 Print or copy a monogram or other design onto paper in your desired size. Iron the slipcover and place a piece of cardboard between the layers where you intend to paint to keep the paint from seeping through. Position dressmaker's carbon paper on the slipcover according to manufacturer's instructions, and place your design on top of the carbon paper. Use a pencil to trace the design (**a**).

2 Remove the carbon paper, and use a paint marker in your desired color or colors to paint the design (**b**), outlining and filling in small sections at a time. Let dry.

3 Use the paint marker to add detailed touches such as dots to the monogram, chair tie, and edges of the slipcover (**c**). Let dry. If desired, heat-set the design using the iron according to the paint marker's instructions so the final design (**d**) will withstand light washing.

tips & tricks

Rather than tracing, look for specialty transfer inkjet paper that lets you print the letter and then iron it onto fabric. Note that this technique will reverse your letter.

Use decorative masking or packing tapes to form random-width stripes on a wall.

Fabric Wrap

From trash to treasure, this delightful perch, *left,* is crafted from a simple wire trash can and a bedsheet. Invert a wire trash can, and screw through the bottom of the can to attach a wood round (found at home improvement stores). Stretch batting and a piece of a sheet or pillowcase across the top of the round, stapling it on the underside using a staple gun. Trim any excess fabric.

Cut a flat sheet into strips, and weave the strips through the can's wires. Knot the ends of each strip in the same place so the knots stack on top of one another to form a decorative element, *above.*

TIP: *The raw edges of the strips on this project will naturally fray. To minimize fraying, apply no-fray glue to the edges.*

Flower Flourishes

Fabric remnants flaunting pretty motifs are hard to part with, even when they're small. Make use of these pieces to adorn a plain upholstered chair or slipcover, *right*.

Apply iron-on adhesive sheets to the back of the fabric using an iron and following manufacturer's directions. Cut out your favorite design elements and discard the excess. Arrange your pieces on the chair or slipcover, and use an iron to adhere them.

TIP: *You can apply iron-on adhesive sheets to solid-color fabrics, too. Then trace or freehand motifs to cut out.*

tips & tricks

Cutting fine lines such as flower stems from iron-on adhesive sheets isn't difficult, but if you find it cumbersome, draw on the lines using a fabric paint marker instead.

Furnish laundry spaces with multitasking cabinets that won't break the bank.

Ironing Board Refresh

Ironing boards rarely need to be replaced, but you might want to update the look with a quick and easy DIY cover.

Remove old cover and lay it flat as a pattern on top of new fabric; cut around. Or lay ironing board on new fabric and cut, adding 3 inches all around.

Turn edges of new fabric under and sew a ½-inch hem all around, leaving an opening on both ends.

Cut a string or ¼-inch elastic band to fit around the board plus several inches, or use the string from the old cover. Attach a safety pin to the elastic or string, and thread it through the hem casing.

Place a new pad on the board, if needed, then slip the cover over top. Cinch tight underneath and tie.

This padded countertop works double time as a folding surface and an ironing surface in one, *this photo.* Plus, there's plenty of storage underneath.

before

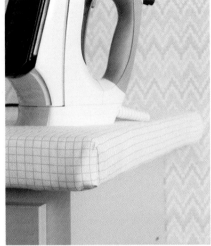

Converted Cabinets

Two kitchen base cabinets ground this ironing center, **opposite**. These cabinets were found at an auction, but look for unfinished stock cabinets at a home improvement center or ask a general contractor for discarded cabinets. They don't even have to match!

Remove hardware and attach two wooden furniture feet, **top, far right,** to the toe-kick of each cabinet. Cut four 1×2 boards to serve as drawer slides for laundry baskets, **above.** Cut the corners from the front of the slides. Attach the boards to the cabinets allowing room to stack two baskets. Prime and paint the cabinets. Let dry.

Place one basket between the cabinets so it rests on the top drawer slide of each cabinet. Measure the distance between the cabinets and remove the basket. Cut a piece of plywood to fit as a counter on top of the cabinets, allowing for a lip of about 1 inch at the front and both sides.

To make the counter suitable for ironing, **top middle,** cut quilt batting and cotton fabric to fit the top of the table plus 3 inches on all sides. Lay fabric right side down on a work surface, and center the batting on top. Place the plywood on the batting. Pull the fabric and batting to the back side of the plywood, pulling taut and stapling to the center of one side and then the opposite side using a staple gun. Repeat with remaining two sides. Continue to secure the fabric and batting all around the plywood. Turn right side up and place on top of the cabinets. Remove drawers and secure the top to the cabinets from underneath.

Complete the work area by cutting cork coasters to serve as laundry basket labels, **above right,** and fashioning an easy-make bag from fabric and an embroidery hoop, **above middle.** To make the bag, sew a pillowcase-style bag from fabric in desired size. Fit open end of the case between the layers of an embroidery hoop that is smaller than the diameter of your case.

materials

before

Sophisticated colors mix with industrial touches to form a modern-day laundry center from an obsolete media cabinet.

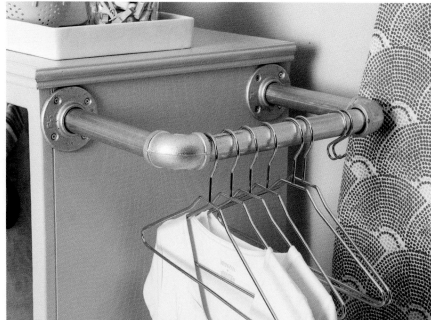

Compact Laundry Center

Create a dream laundry station in just 5 feet of wall space with a flea market media cabinet tailored to make laundry day easier, *opposite*. Remove cabinet knobs, doors, drawers, and shelves. Sand lightly and wipe with a tack cloth. Paint desired color and let dry. Cut a piece of fabric to fit the glass panel, and adhere to the glass using spray adhesive.

Make or purchase cloth laundry bags or make them. These bags are made with two coordinating fabrics and firm fusible stabilizer to keep their form. Each bag features handles and labels, *above* and *far right,* fashioned from recycled leather belts and attached using a leather hole punch, screw posts, and eyelets. Use a white paint marker to write on the leather labels. Add a grommet at the back of the bag and hang using S-hooks.

To make the hanging bars, *right,* use a hacksaw to cut 1 ¼-inch electrical metallic tubing (EMT) conduit pipe to fit the open space, making sure to allow space for a 1 ¼-inch floor flange and 1 ¼-inch elbow on either side. Screw a threaded elbow into a floor flange, and fit the one end of the pipe into the elbow, adhering with metal epoxy per manufacturer's instructions. Repeat for other side. Hold the pipe assembly in place inside the cabinet and attach with screws, using screws long enough to secure the flange but not go through the top of the cabinet (it helps to have an extra set of hands for this).

Follow similar steps to make the clothes bar, *above right,* cutting a length of pipe to fit the cabinet side and two 10-inch pipes to extend out from the cabinet. Fit the pipes into the elbows, and then into the floor flanges, securing each with metal epoxy. Screw the flanges into place on the cabinet.

DARKS

materials

materials

LIGHTS

before

Washtub Wrapping Center

With a few bells and whistles, a vintage double wash tub turns into a gift-wrapping station, *above.* To hold wrapping-paper rolls, drill four holes on each side of the tub, insert eye bolts, and secure with nuts. Place a dowel through a roll of wrapping paper, and then hang from two eye bolts. Repeat with additional rolls, *top left.*

Construct a countertop from MDF to fit the top of the tub, routing out two removable panels to create access to the tub's interior, which is a perfect place to stash a load of ribbons and bows, *bottom left.* Galvanized construction means the tub holds magnet hooks and accessories, too.

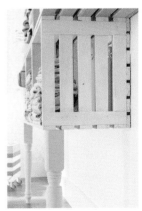

Crate Cubbies

Assorted food crates unite to make a thrifty storage sideboard, *above.* Screw the crates together as desired, then mount to the wall using screws or a French cleat.

Prime and paint furniture legs, then secure them to the crates to support the front, *left.* To expand the top surface areas, cut maple planks to overhang the crates about 10 inches, then screw them to the tops of the crates.

TIP: *To keep fabrics and other supplies tidy, organize them by color in each crate cubby.*

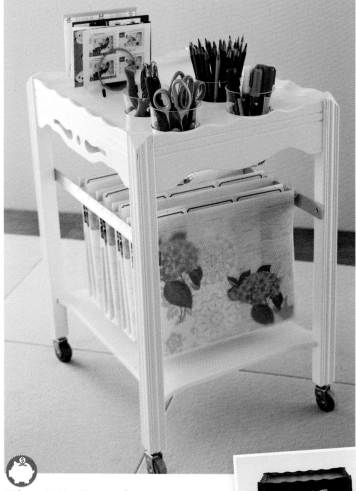

Refashioned Drawer

Scour flea markets for a discarded drawer, *above*. Or rescue a drawer from a piece of furniture destined for the Dumpster. Sand, prime, and paint the drawer. Measure and cut a piece of galvanized metal sheeting to fit inside the drawer. Some hardware stores will cut the sheet to size for you, or use a utility knife and metal straightedge to cut it yourself. Cut decorative paper to the same size and adhere to the metal sheet using spray adhesive. Use construction adhesive to secure the metal to the inside of the drawer.

Attach a picture hanger to the back, and you've got a clever magnetic memo board with built-in shelves on the top and bottom.

Tiny Workstation

Aplenty at thrift shops and garage sales, petite side tables are versatile and easy to upcycle for new uses such as this office cart, *above*. Purchase four tapered water glasses to use as pencil cups. Use a hole saw to cut four holes in the top of the table to hold the glasses. These holes are 3 inches in diameter.

Sand, prime, and paint the table. The space between the legs on this table was just the right width to hold hanging file folders on metal bars screwed into the legs. If your table is too wide, frame out a space 12 ¼ inches wide to accommodate hanging files. Casters are the final touch for this makeover, giving the cart convenient mobility.

before

Outdoor Spaces

Move creativity outside with *sensational seasonal* projects. From *porch to patio*, deck to garden, this chapter promises inspiring makeovers to suit your favorite *open-air retreats.* Get ready for the great outdoors!

Give a basic cedar
potting bench, *this photo,* a
new use as a food and beverage bar. The drawer fronts
were masked with flower
decals and painted blue; the
wood shows through when
the decals are removed. For
hidden storage, clip curtain
rings to a beach towel and
suspend from a tension rod.

Petite Buffet

Small furnishings like this potting table, *right,* can add a lot of value without sacrificing a lot of precious floor space. This petite piece serves up refreshments and stows tabletop and gardening essentials.

To enclose the shelf area, lattice pieces were cut to fit the sides and the back was then secured with screws. The galvanized surface and feet were masked before priming and painting the table hot pink. If your table doesn't have a galvanized surface, have a galvanized sheet cut to fit the top, or cut one yourself using a utility knife and straightedge so the metal ends just short of the edge, and then secure it down using construction adhesive. Don't try to wrap the metal over the edge like this professionally fitted top.

Cup hooks on the side of the table hold garden tools, *below right.* Treat bins to a fun and functional embellishment by stenciling labels on the front, *below, far right.*

tips & tricks

Just as you would protect indoor flooring from furniture legs, consider using casters or plastic furniture sliders so furniture is easier to move and doesn't scratch deck or patio surfaces.

Store and More

Coated with a durable exterior paint, this vintage buffet, *left*, performs double duty as a beverage station and outdoor storage unit for this screened-in room. Colorful new knobs add a touch of color to the front of the crisp white buffet. The bottom drawer was removed for easy access to storage bins.

On top, a fabric runner protects the surface from moisture and scratches, and a vinyl decal mimics a tile backsplash, *above*. Look for easy-to-apply decals that are moisture-resistant. Many decals can be custom-sized to fit your furniture.

TIP: *Wood furniture can expand and contract as temperatures change. Shaving down cabinet doors and drawer fronts can prevent them from sticking.*

Ladder Bench

Vintage stepladders flaunt character and patina that deserve a new purpose. Rather than scrap the rickety relics, refashion them into a quaint outdoor bench, *right* and *below*.

Place the ladders the desired distance apart. For the shelf, cut about eight 1×1 boards to span the distance from the first step of one ladder to the first step of the other ladder. Paint the boards the desired color, and screw them to the step allowing a ½-inch gap in between. Repeat for the seat, cutting boards to secure to the second steps.

For the back, cut trim molding pieces to span the distance from ladder to ladder, and screw to the inside of the ladder legs. **TIP:** *If your seat is longer than 3 feet, brace it in the middle by screwing a 1×4 board underneath from front to back.*

Select a seat or back cushion that blends nicely with the great outdoors.

Hanging Chaise

This large chaise longue, *left,* originally stood on four legs, but hanging it as a swing makes it even more tempting. The legs were removed, and each corner was braced with a galvanized bracket on the outside, *below, far left,* and a block of hardwood on the inside. A hole was drilled through the seat frame and wood block to accommodate a heavy-duty eyebolt, which was secured inside and out with a large washer and nut. Secure eyebolts through beams in the ceiling the same way—though depending on the thickness of your beam, hardwood blocks may not be needed. Secure a carabiner hook to the eyebolt.

Create an eye splice at one end of each rope and thread through a carabiner hook, *above.* Thread the other end of each rope through the hook on the chaise. Raise to desired height and knot. Cut excess rope, and burn the end to seal if using polypropylene rope. Wrap ends with string, if desired. Add comfy pillows, *left,* and then kick back and relax.

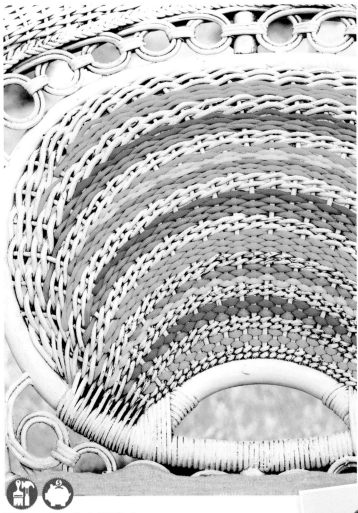

Wonderful Wicker

A dated wicker chair might seem undesirable, but a few cosmetic touches will have it looking high-style in no time, *opposite*. If it's dusty, vacuum to clean the surface and grooves. Prep the chair, sand it, wipe with a damp cloth, and let dry. Paint the chair with two coats of white. If using spray paint or a sprayer, use various angles to get into the weaving. If using a paintbrush, use a pouncing motion and generous amount of paint to get into hard-to-reach crevices. Paint the underside of the chair first. Select areas to accent with contrasting paint color, like the blue used on the side of this chair, *above right*. Thread neon cord or twine through back side of chair, alternating colors, *above*. Find a wicker chair with a design with some open spaces in the weaving to accommodate the cord. Use a large-eye needle to thread the cord through, or tape an end of cord with masking tape and thread that through. Tie the loose ends in the back, and trim excess.

    Use the original cushion as a pattern to cut new upholstery foam for the seat cushion. Sew a cover from desired fabric.

before

materials

tips & tricks

If the wicker has a glossy finish, consider using a liquid deglosser before painting to help the paint adhere well to the surface.

A dowdy wicker chair enjoys a fresh outlook with crisp white paint, vibrant woven accents, and a seat cover flaunting a modern geometric print, *this photo*.

Refashioned Folding Chair

Don't be intimidated by metal furnishings. Follow these steps for a fabulous facelift.

materials

- Drop cloth
- Scrub brush
- Bucket
- Dish soap
- Wire brush
- Steel wool
- Rust-inhibiting spray primer
- Spray paint
- Clear gloss enamel spray paint

instructions

1 Gather materials (*a*). Working over a drop cloth, dip a scrub brush in soapy water and scrub the chair to remove dirt, grease, and other residue (*b*).

2 Repeat Step 1 with a wire brush and then steel wool (*c*). Rinse with soapy water and allow to dry.

3 Apply a coat of rust-inhibiting spray primer (*d*). Allow the primer to dry overnight before painting the chair. For best results, let paint dry for 24 hours between coats.

4 Finish with a coat or two of clear gloss enamel.

Park Bench Perk-Up

A basic slatted park bench gets a big boost with paint, cushions, and an angled edge detail, *left*. Use a hacksaw to cut the corners from the top and bottom planks on the bench back and from the front of the seat. Use a hand sander to round the edges. Prime and paint the bench desired color. Let dry.

Purchase or sew a boxed seat cushion from outdoor fabrics, *below*, making sure the cushion insert is also suited for the outdoors.

Texture Treatment

Lacking personal style, this drab green bench needed a lift. A Provence blue hue came to the rescue along with a raised texture to add a load of charming character, *left* and *opposite.* The texture is created with a tintable plaster product called Fine Stone, which is suitable for indoor and outdoor use.

Start by giving the bench a blue base coat and let dry. Cut lace pieces to fit partway down each slatted section on the bench back. Spray the back of a piece of lace with stencil adhesive, and apply to the first slat. Apply Fine Stone product over the lace using a trowel, pushing it through the lace and smoothing it out to about ⅛-inch thickness. Remove the lace and repeat with new lace pieces on remaining slats, the bench apron, and fronts of legs. If you aren't happy with how the stone transfers to a section, scrape it off immediately and try again.

When dry, lightly sand to buff the edges of the raised texture. For added dimension, consider using a dry brush to apply a small amount of lighter blue paint over the stenciled section, and then sand lightly. Follow the same steps to add stenciled texture to the bottom part of the slats, overlapping the lace stencil 2–4 inches. Let dry, and finish the entire bench with clear polyurethane.

TIP: *Experiment with various laces or stencils on a scrap of wood. Surprisingly, thinner, more delicate lace works better for this application than heavier lace.*

before

materials

tips & tricks

The sandstone treatment results in a rough texture. Be sure to sand it lightly to remove edges that could snag clothing.

Give a wooden garden bench a soft style, *this photo*, with a delicate lace stencil and a charming blue hue. Apply the pattern generously or to just a few accent areas.

Painted Metal

When searching for metal garden chairs, a little rust and a few small dents are OK, but avoid those with excessive rust or dents, which just can't be fixed with paint. Sand away small rust spots, and then wipe the chair with a tack cloth. Prime using a rust-inhibiting primer and let dry. Apply the top coat of your choice. Metallic silver spray paint was used on this chair, *above* and *opposite.*

Purchase, crochet, or knit flower embellishments for the chair back, and tie them on with string through the open slats.

TIP: *If you want a professional-grade finish, talk to an auto-body shop or have the chair powder-coated.*

Upholstery Update

This chair's curvaceous figure, ***above*** and ***opposite,*** was too charming to pass up, but the original ruby red fabric was faded and worn. The solution? Chic new upholstery in unexpected patterns and colors. The original fabric was removed and the chair frame was primed and painted with semigloss latex paint, and then allowed to dry.

The new fabric was cut to fit (using the old fabric as a pattern) and applied to the chair over a layer of fresh batting on the seat and back. A coordinating pattern was used on the back and arms of the chair. Ivory gimp and silver nailheads add irresistible detail around the edges.

TIP: *If you fall in love with fabrics that aren't constructed for outdoor use, never fear. Coat them with a waterproofing protectant spray.*

Pair hand-me-downs and flea market finds to create an eclectic outdoor setting, *this photo,* that doesn't cost a fortune. New fabric and paint finishes help unite various styles.

Yarn-bomb a vintage bike to create a quirky artwork sculpture.

Boosted Bench

No need to build a porch swing from scratch when you can start with a garden bench. The legs were cut off this bench, *right,* and 2×4 boards were screwed underneath at the front and back of the bench, long enough to extend beyond the sides about 5 inches. A piece of decorative rope molding was glued to the front board.

A hole was drilled in each board about 3 inches from each end as well as in the arm of the bench directly above, and then the bench was painted a happy yellow hue. To hang the bench, two S hooks placed at each rope's center were attached to an eyebolt in the ceiling, *above left,* and the ends of the rope were threaded through the holes and knotted underneath. A magazine rack conveniently holds easy reads on the side of the bench, *above right.*

Small accent tables are a nice way to add DIY style to decks and patios.

Painted Pattern

Nautical themes are a natural for outdoor spaces, and this blue metal stool, *above,* was a perfect canvas for a stylized fishnet pattern. Apply the pattern using a white paint marker, freehanding the top row first and working your way down. Imperfect lines are acceptable, and even preferable, for this free-flowing design. If you prefer a more perfect composition, however, you can cut a template from cardboard and trace around it.

TIP: *If a stool doesn't provide a large enough tabletop for your needs, buy a small table round or cut one from wood or MDF, and attach it to the stool using construction adhesive. Just be sure the top isn't too large for the stool to support.*

Rope Covering

Disguise a basic fiberboard table with a trendy rope cover, *above.* Nail the ends of two types of sisal rope to the center of the tabletop. Apply construction adhesive around the nailed ends to secure. Continue to apply adhesive in a spiral around the center while winding and securing the ropes, *right,* to cover the entire top and over the table edge, occasionally tacking the ropes with nails.

Repeat to cover the base, using construction adhesive, wrapping, and nailing to secure the rope, *right*. To make joins, nail the end of the new rope to an edge of the table, leaving about an inch to tuck behind the previous round of rope. Bring the new rope end up from behind the previous round, nailing to the edge before continuing to wind around the base. Attach the tabletop to the base, and coat the table with a clear sealer.

Transform a few shipping pallets
into an eco-chic coffee table, *this photo,* painted with
durable exterior paint. Integrate a flower box, *opposite,*
filled with low-maintenance Scotch moss, which will
last for several months.

Recycled Pallet Table

Recycled and repurposed shipping pallets are the main ingredient for this Earth-friendly project.

materials

- Two wooden pallets
- Planter box
- Measuring tape
- Framing square
- Saber saw
- 100-grit sandpaper
- Eight mending plates
- 24 wood screws (1 ¼-inch)
- Drill
- Four concrete half-blocks
- Paintbrush
- Primer
- Exterior paint

instructions

1 To cut a hole for the planter, use the long edge of the planter box as a guide; draw the first cut line on the top pallet (*a*). Measure the width of the planter at its widest: just below the lip (*b*). Transfer that measurement to mark the second cut line (*c*).

2 Using the framing square, draw the third and fourth cut lines on the pallet parallel to the first two lines (*d*).

3 Cut an opening in the top pallet for the planter box using a saber saw and following the cut lines (*e*). Sand the edges of the opening.

4 Stack the pallets bottom to bottom. Position a mending plate near the outside corners of the pallets and mark holes (*f*). Drill pilot holes, then use wood screws to attach the plates, securing the pallets together.

5 Apply primer to the concrete half-blocks and to the pallets; let dry overnight. Apply one or two coats of exterior-grade paint to the blocks and the pallet. When dry, place a block under each corner of the pallet to raise it to coffee-table height.

materials

a

b

c

d

e

f

Green and blue hues allow furniture projects to blend with outdoor settings.

Table Refresh

This perfect little coffee table, **right,** started as a perfect little dining table, but that wasn't what this screened porch needed. So the base was removed, cut down to coffee-table height, and reattached. Then the table was painted a cool sky blue.

Oversize nailheads with a polished-chrome finish, **below,** were tapped in around the apron. To help keep the nailheads level, run a strip of tape along the apron so one edge is at the apron's center. Draw a light pencil line along that edge and remove the tape. Be sure to tap each nail into that line. To space the nailheads consistently, measure and mark the placement from nail to nail, use a nailhead-spacer tool, or—if time trumps perfection—just eyeball it.

For a fun pillow, trace and fill in butterfly shapes using a fabric marker.

Industrial Table

The original purpose of this steel factory frame wasn't exactly clear, but it was clearly a perfect piece to upcycle as a coffee table. To preserve the frame's painted patina, it was coated with a clear polyurethane.

A piece of maple plywood was cut to fit into the recessed frame and stained a dark cherry color. When dry, three large alliums were stenciled atop the stain, *above*. To protect the stained and painted surface from water marks and scratches, several coats of spar varnish were applied, and casters were added to make moving the heavy table a snap.

TIP: *Many varnishes will yellow stained or painted surfaces. Test a scrap piece before varnishing your project.*

gallery of great ideas
Add personal style to outdoor spaces with doable projects big and small.

Whether vintage or new, most iron garden furniture sports a finish in black or bronze—not too perky for a festive outdoor space. Metal primer and bold paint colors such as sunny yellow and turquoise, *above,* switch things up in a flash. Give dowdy cushions new colorful covers, too!

A step stool is certainly a handy helper, but it's a snap to boost its capabilities even more. First paint the bench to suit your taste. Add hooks to each side of the stool, and secure a garden belt to the back, *above.* Look for stools with a convenient hand grip in the top, or cut one out yourself using a jigsaw.

Show your stripes with this playful chair, *above.* Clean the wicker, then paint it red using outdoor paint. Place 1-inch painter's tape every inch across the chair seat and back. Paint wicker between the tape desired colors. Remove tape and let dry. Mask painted stripes with painter's tape, and paint wicker between the tape in desired colors. Leave a few stripes red, if desired. Remove tape; let dry.

Here's one way to reinvent the wheel—upcycle a tire into a storage table, *above.* Cut a circular base from MDF. Wash the tire thoroughly. Prime the tire and base with oil-base primer, and then paint with latex outdoor paint. Add casters to base and secure to tire with construction adhesive. Construct a top from cedar planks.

Versatile and eco-chic, tree-trunk sections, *above,* serve as handy side tables or stools. Use a chainsaw to cut the trunks to desired height, and then sand smooth. Make them easy to move around your outdoor space by securing casters or plastic furniture sliders underneath.

Turn a small vintage kitchen island into a garden station, *above.* For a handy soil container, cut a hole in the tabletop to fit a lidded casserole dish. If there is no lower shelf, add 1×3 boards to the table legs and secure wooden planks across them. Add hooks to the side of the table for hanging various garden tools.

Fountain Table

A small metal table becomes a soothing fountain, *left*, by swapping the glass top for a plastic planter bowl. Find a waterproof bowl with a lip to fit inside the table frame. If you can't find one to fit, leave the tabletop on and place the bowl on top of the table. To bring water to life, place a submersible pump in the bowl and attach a fountain. Conceal the pump by placing glass balls in the bowl and running the electrical cord down the table leg. Add water and plug the pump into a grounded outlet according to manufacturer instructions. Replenish water as it evaporates, keeping the pump submerged to ensure it works properly.

TIP: *As an alternative to glass balls, you could use pretty stones, shells, marbles, or driftwood.*

tips & tricks
Most pump cords are black, so consider wrapping the cord with white duct tape so it's less noticeable inside the container.

Furniture makeovers don't get much more dramatic than this! A kitchen cupboard, *this photo,* was in such sad shape it was being given away. Lime green and perky pink paint kick-start the redo, while a tiled surface, *middle left,* and hardworking organizers, *top left* and *bottom left,* make it a top-notch potting bench.

Tile a Tabletop

Mosaic tiles add fun color and style to this garden center.
Plus, they are durable and easy to clean.

materials

- Exterior-grade plywood
- Drill, screws, and mixer attachment
- 1-inch wood trim
- Wood glue
- Paint and paintbrush
- Notched trowel
- Thinset adhesive
- Ceramic tile
- Grout mix
- Plastic bucket
- Rubber float
- Sponge
- Grout sealer

instructions

1 Cut plywood to fit the cabinet work surface. Screw plywood to the cabinet base. Cut wood trim to fit sides of plywood, and secure to sides using wood glue, creating a ½-inch lip. Paint and let dry.

2 Use a notched trowel to apply thinset adhesive to the top of the plywood (***a***). Place tile on the adhesive (***b***). Let dry for 24 hours.

3 Mix grout according to package directions (***c***). To grout the joints, use a rubber float to spread the grout mix over the surface (***d***). Once the grout is firm, use a damp sponge to wipe off excess (***e***).

4 Allow the grout to set for 24 hours (***f***). Apply grout sealer according to package directions.

before

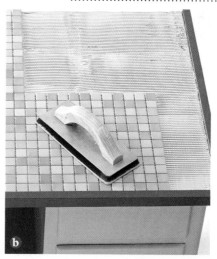

Tools & Techniques

Dig in to the following *hardworking pages* for priceless *tips and tricks* sure to make your next furniture project magnificent. Get all the know-how for *tried-and-true* tools and techniques, and then let your creative visions come to life.

The Hunt

Whether you're perusing flea markets, *left*, for diamonds in the rough, or you're thinking of refreshing furniture you already own, here's what to look for in furniture makeover candidates:

Character: Choose furniture with interesting lines, charming personality, or unique details. Find a piece you love and are inspired to renew.

Condition: No matter how much character a piece has, it's got to be sturdy and in need of few, easy, and inexpensive repairs (think sanding, gluing, painting). Opt for solid, secure joints; rickety ones could mean disassembling and regluing the whole piece, which is major work. Avoid furniture with damaged legs or pieces that smell like smoke or mildew, because those can be difficult to fix.

Construction: Look the piece over inside and out to see how it's assembled. Do the frame and drawers have solid joints? Dovetail joints are a plus! Do the drawers slide smoothly on wooden runners? If the piece is heavy, that's a good sign. Quality, well-built pieces will last and are worth your time.

Material: Determine if the piece is solid wood. If so, what kind—quartersawn oak, walnut, knotty pine? Different woods will take paint and stain differently. Wood veneers have potential if in good shape. Laminates can be tricky and perhaps not the best choice for a makeover.

10 painting tips

1. **Test your paint color** before committing the hue to the entire piece. Paint the furniture back or a sample board, let it dry, and place it in different lights to make sure you like it.

2. **There's a difference between dry time,** when paint is dry to the touch, and cure time, when the finish is durable. It can take several days to weeks for paint to fully cure, and humidity can extend that time.

3. **To determine whether a painted surface** was painted with an oil- or water-base paint, soak a cotton ball in ammonia and stick it to the surface using painter's tape. Remove after an hour; if the painted surface has wrinkles, it's water-base paint.

4. **Apply no more than 8–10 inches** of painter's tape at a time to help assure a straight edge. Smooth the edges with a putty knife. Remove the tape when the paint is dry to the touch but slightly tacky, pulling it up slowly at a 45-degree angle. If it sticks, loosen it from the paint by running a crafts knife along the seam.

5. **When sealing a painted surface,** use an oil-base sealer over oil-base paint. Both oil- and latex-base sealers can be used over latex paint.

6. **If you take a break from the project,** wrap your brush in plastic bags, squeezing out the air and sealing with twist ties or rubber bands.

7. **Assess the furniture and prep it accordingly.** For some pieces, a good wipe-down may do the trick. But many furnishings need to be sanded, filled, and primed before the surface is ready for a new coat of paint.

8. **Use a quality brush that** applies paint smoothly and doesn't leave stray bristles behind. Bristles should be slightly longer in the center than on the edge and be bound to a wooden handle with a nailed-on, rust-resistant metal ferrule.

9. **Remove all hardware before painting.** If the piece has hinges, be sure to mark their corresponding door and location so that it's easy to replace them in their original spots. While replacing old knobs and pulls is an easy upgrade, old hinges are harder to match, so be sure you can find replacements that work before tossing the original ones.

10. **Start painting at the top** of a piece and work your way down, feathering in the paint and blending in any drips.

spray painting

A grip handle turns an aerosol can into a handy spray gun, minimizing finger fatigue and messes. Prevent clogging of any spray-paint can valve by holding the can upside down and spraying until only a clear gas is released. If the tip becomes clogged, wipe off the opening with warm water or lacquer thinner. Never stick a pin or wire into the hole.

see the sheen

Flat
Flat paint has a matte finish that's pretty much nonreflective, which is good for hiding blemishes like bumps or small cracks. This finish does show scuffs and marks and is harder to clean. This sheen is not commonly used on furniture.

Satin or Eggshell
Satin or eggshell paint shows a slight luster and falls in the just-right category—not too shiny, not too dull. It's more durable than flat paint and easier to clean.

Semigloss
Semigloss paint has a tougher skin and higher luster than satin and eggshell paints and is a common choice for furniture. It cleans up and wears well, but because it reflects more light when dry, it shows more imperfections.

Gloss
Gloss paint creates a hard, shiny luster that is durable and easy to clean. It gives furnishings a modern, lacquered appearance. It's long-lasting, but it will make imperfections clearly visible, so proper prep work is very important.

how to paint anything

To paint any surface right, consider these tips and research specialty products.

LAMINATE

To paint laminate surfaces, *above,* successfully, clean the surface with water and mild detergent. Let dry, and then sand with low-grit sandpaper. Wipe with a tack cloth to remove dust. To improve the paint's adhesion, apply a bonding primer suitable for laminate surfaces. Let dry according to the manufacturer's directions. Roll or spray on a top coat of paint that is compatible with the primer. Consider testing a hidden spot first.

UNFINISHED WOOD

Unfinished wood furniture, *above,* is usually ready to paint. However, if the piece isn't smooth, sand nicks or scratches going in the direction of the wood grain. Smooth the surface with fine sandpaper, and remove the dust using a tack cloth. Prime the piece, going in the direction of the grain; paint sticks better to primer than it does to raw wood. Let dry, and then lightly sand and remove dust. Brush or roll paint in the direction of the wood grain. Let paint dry and cure before use.

PLASTIC

When painting plastic, *above,* sand the surface lightly to improve adhesion. Wash with trisodium phosphate. Be careful not to touch the clean surface, because that leaves oil behind. Apply spray primer, then spray paint, both designed for plastic. Or brush on a paint formulated for plastic, which is designed to bond to plastic without priming. Apply multiple thin coats, letting dry between coats.

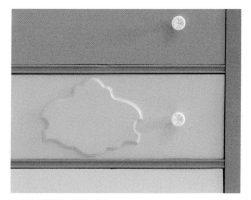

WICKER

Spray-painting is the easiest way to refresh wicker, *above.* Synthetic or all-weather wicker is made of resin, a type of plastic. Therefore, spray with a paint formulated for plastic, or apply a primer for plastic first, and then an outdoor acrylic spray paint. For traditional wicker, use oil-base spray paint. Clean and prep the wicker well, and spray from different angles to get into all of the nooks and crannies of the weaving.

PAINTED WOOD

Remove dirt or wax buildup from painted wood, *above,* using a household cleaner; rinse. Sand rough areas, and wipe away dust with a tack cloth. Apply two coats of stain-blocking primer, letting dry between coats. Roll or brush on two coats of paint, starting at the top. For durability, use a semigloss or gloss finish in latex or oil-base paint. Make sure the type of primer you choose is compatible with the paint. Oil-base paints require oil-base primers. Let dry and sit undisturbed until cured.

METAL

Clean a metal surface, *above,* with a stiff wire brush to remove flaking paint or rust. Wipe down with a mixture of bleach and water; let dry. Prime with a metal primer and let dry, or use a paint formulated with rust inhibitors. Apply several thin coats of paint. If using spray paint, hold the can 10–12 inches from the surface as you spray. Shake the can during application to keep the color mixed, and spray lightly to avoid paint runs. Let cure before use.

the right stuff

PLASTIC AND CANVAS DROP CLOTH Drop cloths protect your work surface. Canvas cloths absorb liquid and are heavy enough to stay put when used on the floor or over furniture. A tight weave offers the best protection. Plastic cloths are inexpensive, but they don't absorb paint, can be slippery, and may shift.

Use this essential tool for opening cans of paint without ruining the lid.

STIR STICKS Grab free sticks when you buy paint. Stir paint thoroughly and frequently to keep the color evenly mixed.

Use lint-free cloths to remove dust, clean spills, and wipe away mistakes.

PAINTER'S TAPE Available in various widths, painter's tape is used to mask off areas before painting. Medium-adhesion tape is often used on wood with a nonporous finish, such as gloss or semigloss paint. Low-tack tape is good for delicate surfaces and less likely to pull off paint when removed.

know your paintbrushes

3-INCH BRUSH Good for painting larger areas, hold it between your thumb and fingers in a relaxed grip.

ANGLED BRUSH This is the best brush for painting furniture edges or where you need more control. Hold it like a pencil.

HOUSEHOLD BRUSH Perfect for painting small areas.

FOAM BRUSH Available in a variety of sizes, these brushes are disposable and great for craft projects.

ARTIST'S BRUSHES These work nicely for detail work and freehand designs.

STENCIL BRUSH Stencil brushes are available in a variety of sizes. Use large ones for overall coverage and small ones to fill in details.

WEAVER BRUSH A weaver brush is used to create the look of linen or denim.

painter's pyramids

These innovative, inexpensive little nonstick tools securely elevate your project off the work surface when painting, staining, or gluing, which means better access to edges, no sticking to the work surface, less mess, and less project time!

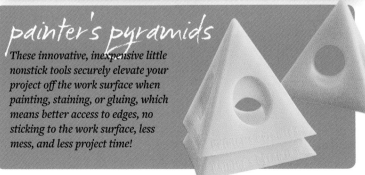

special finishes
If you're craving something more than color, venture beyond standard paint. These specialty coatings deliver custom results with little effort.

WOOD STAIN - MINWAX Highlight the beauty of a wood's grain with traditional wood-tone or color stain, and then protect the stain with a gloss or satin polyurethane.

DRY-ERASE PAINT - RUST-OLEUM Create a message board on the side of a cabinet, using dry-erase paint, which is sold as a two-part formula.

CHALKBOARD PAINT - KRYLON Make furniture surfaces writable and erasable using this specialty paint, which comes in black as well as other colors.

CRACKLE VARNISH - ANNIE SLOAN Let crackle varnish give furnishings an aged look with a crackled, weathered patina.

GLITTER SPRAY PAINT - KRYLON Spray on an intense sparkling effect with this glamorous formula.

METALLIC PAINT - KRYLON Paint on a beautiful metallic shimmer while also inhibiting rust.

MAGNETIC PAINT - RUST-OLEUM Combine a magnetic primer with your favorite latex or spray colors for a painted surface that multitasks.

TEXTURE PAINT - BENJAMIN MOORE Create a personalized surface with sand-texture paint tinted to your favorite hue.

PAINT AND PRIMER IN ONE - OLYMPIC Cut a two-step process in half with tintable formulas that blend paint and primer in one can.

CHALK PAINT - ANNIE SLOAN Achieve a gorgeous painted surface with chalky colors and a rubbed-on layer of protective wax.

GLITTER OVERLAY - BENJAMIN MOORE Add a glittering effect to any painted surface with this easy-to-apply top coat.

faux wood grain
Treat a dresser top to an easy-do faux bois finish using a wood-graining tool.

Prime the dresser and let dry. Paint the dresser turquoise (or desired color). When dry, use painter's tape to mask off the dresser top.

In a plastic container, mix 4 parts glaze medium with 1 part white paint. You'll need enough glaze to equal the amount of one coat of base color to cover the dresser top. Pour the glaze mixture on a paper plate, and roll a narrow width of it on the dresser using a foam roller.

Working quickly, start at one side and pull the wood-graining tool across the dresser, creating a plank effect. As you pull the tool, rock it back and forth to vary the texture. After one pass, repeat to make a second "plank" that slightly overlaps the first.

Continue across the entire dresser top, reloading the tool with the glaze mixture and cleaning the excess glaze from the tool as you go. Remove the tape and let dry. Apply two coats of finish sealer. Let dry, and then top with your favorite accessories.

Clean the wood-graining tool thoroughly with warm soapy water, removing paint from the notched surface.

wallpapering

A roll of wallpaper can add a pop of fun color or high-end style to furniture. Look for wallpaper remnants or partially used rolls and the project will cost you next to nothing. Measure the surface to be papered, and cut paper to size. Or you can cut paper slightly larger and trim excess later. Be sure to match the pattern, if needed.

Remove any hardware, such as the drawer pulls on this dresser, *below*. Use wallpaper paste or heavy-duty spray adhesive to attach the wallpaper to the surface, following adhesive directions. When wallpapering drawer fronts, remove drawers from the dresser. Smooth paper as you go to remove air pockets. Let dry. Replace hardware, if needed.

To match a wallpaper pattern over multiple drawers, cut one piece to cover all drawers, tape in place, then mark excess to remove.

upholstering tips

Upholstering furniture takes time and a few specialty tools, but it's definitely worth the cost savings and DIY bragging rights.

Take photos of your furniture from all angles and of joints and connections of seats, arms, and back before you start stripping it. You'll want to refer to them later when you're reassembling things.

Keep all upholstery and padding that you remove to use as patterns when you cut new upholstery and padding. Discard the old upholstery after the piece is done.

Old furniture is often dirty and dusty, so wear a dust mask and safety glasses while stripping off fabric to keep airborne particles out of your lungs and eyes. Wear work gloves to protect your hands from staples and splinters, and shoes to keep from stepping on any that have dropped to the floor.

Select high-quality upholstery foam and batting. If you're investing the time and money to reupholster a piece, don't skimp on the foam or it won't be comfortable.

Consider the shape of your furniture when selecting new fabric. Stripes and patterns can stretch and not match up well. Consider solids with texture for interest or overall small-scale patterns.

A hot-glue gun is a nice little tool to secure trim pieces or even the upholstery in hard-to-reach places, such as between arms and seats.

If you're going to paint the frame, do so once the piece has been stripped but not yet reupholstered. Painting after it's upholstered means a lot of masking to protect the fabric and makes it harder to apply paint to hard-to-reach areas.

Select durable, stain-resistant fabrics, or apply a stain blocker on fabric before you upholster so you don't have to mask your frame to treat it afterward.

natural beauty Paint is a great makeover solution, but it may not be right for every piece of furniture. Rescue hardwood pieces such as this dresser, *right*, from layers of paint by stripping and then staining to reveal lustrous graining and natural wood hues.

Refinishing Wood

Follow these steps to restore painted wood furnishings with a better-than-new finish.

materials

- Drop cloth
- Nitrile gloves
- Respirator
- Wood stripper
- 2- or 4-inch foam brushes
- 2- or 3-inch putty knives
- Scrap bucket
- Small wire-bristle brushes
- Steel wool
- Mineral spirits
- Medium (80–60) and fine (200–100) sandpaper
- Tack cloths
- Stain and stirrer
- Paintbrush or staining pad
- Cheesecloth
- Water-base polyurethane
- Spray paint

before

instructions

1 Remove drawers and hardware from dresser. Place on a leak-proof drop cloth in a ventilated area. Wearing gloves and respirator, following manufacturer instructions, and using a foam brush, apply a ⅛-inch-thick layer of wood stripper (*a*).

2 Once the surface has bubbled, use a plastic putty knife to scrape off paint (*b*); discard paint remnants in a scrap bucket. Repeat if needed. Use a small wire-bristle brush to remove paint from crevices (*c*).

3 Using a piece of steel wool and rubbing with the direction of the grain, wipe down the wood with mineral spirits to remove stripper and paint residue (*d*). Allow to dry 15 minutes. Sand the dresser using a medium-grit sandpaper, moving with even pressure and in the direction of the grain. Wipe with a tack cloth. Sand again with a fine-grit sandpaper and wipe with a tack cloth.

4 Thoroughly stir stain and, using a paintbrush or staining pad and following manufacturer instructions, apply stain, working in the direction of the grain and completing small areas at a time (*e*). After applying stain in one section, wait about 5 minutes and wipe with cheesecloth to remove excess (*f*). Continue applying stain to the rest of the dresser. If a darker color is desired, repeat staining steps.

5 Wipe down the dresser with a clean tack cloth. Working first on the horizontal surface, drizzle a light line of polyurethane onto the dresser. Spread in the direction of the grain using a bristle brush, working quickly and brushing over the same area only as much as needed to avoid bubbles, streaks, and imperfections. Cover the entire dresser and let dry 12–24 hours.

6 If a second coat of polyurethane is desired or imperfections appear, lightly sand with very fine-grit sandpaper, wipe with a tack cloth, and repeat the polyurethane process. Spray-paint the hardware, allow to dry thoroughly, and reinstall.

stenciling

If freehand isn't your forte, stencils are a supereasy way to achieve perfect-looking designs in no time, *below.* There are stencils in endless styles, patterns, and sizes, or you can cut your own from stencil paper.

Successful Stenciling

The hardest part of stenciling is choosing a design! Look online for inspiration and products, and be sure the stencil you select fits your furniture.

materials

- Stencil
- Stencil adhesive or painter's tape
- Paint
- Plastic plate
- Stencil brush
- Paper towels
- Polyurethane

instructions

1 Plan out your design. You might offset the design, apply it to the front rather than the top surface, or repeat the design multiple times.

2 Spray the stencil back with stencil adhesive or secure it to the surface using painter's tape.

3 Pour a small amount of paint on a plastic plate. Dip a stencil brush into the paint, and dab excess on a paper towel. Gently apply the paint to the stenciled area with a dabbing motion. Use light pressure, and apply a few light coats rather than thick ones. If repeating the design, remove the stencil, wipe it off, and reposition using the stencil's registration marks. Let dry completely. Apply clear polyurethane.

metal leafing

Traditionally called gilding, this lustrous technique, *below,* has been around for years, often used on picture frames and artwork. Metal leafing kits are available at crafts stores and can be applied to painted surfaces (on top of the paint or underneath paint, which is then sanded to let the leafing show through) or unpainted surfaces.

Determine where you want the metal leafing on your furniture. Apply the adhesive to the exact area using a small crafts brush. Let the adhesive set up according to manufacturer's instructions. Once set, carefully apply sheets of metal leaf to the adhesive one sheet at a time and overlapping slightly. Smooth out the sheets using fingertips and a soft-bristle brush to flatten wrinkles as you go, and brush away excess metal leaf. Once covered, apply a clear sealer over the metal leaf to protect it and keep it from oxidizing.

paper accents

Used for centuries, decoupage techniques apply a varnish or lacquer to adhere paper (or fabric or other flat materials) to furniture, ***below right,*** and other surfaces. Crafts glues are typically used for modern-day decoupage, making for quick and easy projects with big results.

Decorating with Decoupage

If you can cut and paste, you can decoupage. Use it on individual or overlapping cutouts, or an entire surface.

materials

- Paper (wrapping paper, scrapbook paper, maps, newspaper, sheet music, vintage paper ephemera, art paper, calendar artwork, illustrations, etc.)
- Scissors or crafts knife
- Shallow tray of water
- Decoupage medium such as Mod Podge
- Foam crafts brush
- Damp paper towels
- Polyurethane

instructions

1 Make sure your furniture piece is smooth. Repair any bumps or gouges. Wipe furniture surface clean and let dry. Plan your design and select papers. Don't use images printed on an ink-jet printer, as the color will run. Laser-printed images work fine. Cut out paper designs (***a***).

2 Place one paper design into a tray of water (***b***). Let sit about 10 seconds or until edges start to curl. Thicker paper can soak slightly longer. Some decoupage methods skip this soaking step and just apply decoupage medium to the back of the paper design. Experiment to see which method works best for you.

3 Brush decoupage medium onto furniture surface (***c***) and place your paper design on top, smoothing with your fingers (***d***). Apply more medium over top (***e***). Repeat with all paper designs, cleaning fingers with damp paper towels when needed; then let dry thoroughly. Seal entire surface with two coats polyurethane, sanding and letting dry between coats.

Retrofitting a Sink

Transforming a dresser or buffet into a bathroom vanity is rewarding and doable with a few common tools.

materials

- Sink and faucet
- Positioning template (if your sink doesn't come with one, trace the sink outline and create one with paper)
- Tape
- Pencil or marker
- Jigsaw

instructions

1 Remove the drawers and any drawer supports that will interfere with the plumbing. Decide where you want the sink to be placed on the dresser top. Tape the positioning template in the desired place; trace (**a**). If you will be mounting the faucet outside the sink, as in this example, mark its placement.

2 Determine the location of the water supply and drain lines. Mark this location on the back of the dresser. Using a jigsaw, cut the sink, faucet, and water supply/drain line openings (**b**).

3 Set the sink and faucet in place, following the manufacturer's instructions. Hook up the plumbing. Use the jigsaw to cut the backs of the drawers that surround the sink and/or plumbing so they fit into place (**c**). Insert the drawers.

4 If you are skilled at plumbing, hook up the plumbing yourself (**d**); otherwise, hire a professional plumber.

assembling your toolbox

RUBBER MALLET
Use this tool if a standard hammer would damage the surface you are striking.

CLAW HAMMER
Available in a range of weights depending on your task. The claw makes nail-pulling easy.

RANDOM-ORBIT SANDER
When hand-sanding isn't enough, use this tool to smooth surfaces.

SANDPAPER & SANDING BLOCK
Available in various grits, use these for smoothing repairs and prepping furniture.

DUST MASK
Wear protective gear (dust mask and safety glasses) to avoid harmful particles getting into lungs or eyes.

PLIERS
Stock up on a variety of pliers, such as linesman's, long-nose, locking, and tongue-and-groove styles.

JIGSAW
This power tool is lightweight, is easy to use, and allows controlled intricate or curved cuts.

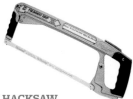

HACKSAW
A workhorse with various blades to cut metal, plastic, or other hard materials or softer materials.

CIRCULAR SAW
Nice for larger-scale projects, this saw is designed for fast, smooth, accurate cuts in lumber and plywood.

BACKSAW & MITER BOX
Good for precision work such as cutting 90- or 45-degree angles.

UTILITY KNIFE
A staple for any toolbox, this knife can cut just about anything for your various DIY projects.

STAPLE GUN
This tool uses a spring-loaded striker to drive a staple or brad nail into wood or other materials.

SCREWDRIVERS
Choose a variety of Phillips and flat-head screwdrivers, or a ratcheting model with interchangeable heads.

TAPE MEASURE
Look for tapes with a locking blade, belt clip, and sturdy case. Smaller ones are lighter and easier to carry around.

CORDLESS DRILL-DRIVER
A DIY must-have. Drill holes and drive fasteners quickly and precisely.

PUTTY KNIVES
Stock up on a variety of scrapers and putty knives, and add an indispensable 5-in-1 tool as well.

HOT-GLUE GUN
Often reserved for smaller crafts projects, this tool can tackle larger jobs with its fast-setting adhesive.

CLAMPS
From spring clamps to bar clamps, several varieties will come in handy for big and small DIY projects.

WOOD GLUE
This adhesive makes repairs in wood that are super-strong and virtually invisible when done right.

WOOD FILLER
For small wood repairs, this compound fills dents and imperfections, and it can be sanded smooth and painted.

INDEX